WhatsApp and Everyday Life
in West Africa

WhatsApp and Everyday Life in West Africa

Beyond Fake News

Edited by
Idayat Hassan and Jamie Hitchen

ZED

LONDON • NEW YORK • OXFORD • NEW DELHI • SYDNEY

ZED BOOKS
Bloomsbury Publishing Plc
50 Bedford Square, London, WC1B 3DP, UK
1385 Broadway, New York, NY 10018, USA
29 Earlsfort Terrace, Dublin 2, Ireland

BLOOMSBURY and Zed Books are trademarks of Bloomsbury Publishing Plc

First published in Great Britain 2022

A catalogue record for this book is available from the British Library.

Library of Congress Cataloging-in-Publication Data
Names: Hassan, Idayat, editor. | Hitchen, Jamie, editor.
Title: WhatsApp and everyday life in West Africa: beyond fake news /
edited by Idayat Hassan and Jamie Hitchen.
Description: New York: Zed Books, an imprint of Bloomsbury Publishing, 2022. |
Includes bibliographical references and index.
Identifiers: LCCN 2022003854 (print) | LCCN 2022003855 (ebook) |
ISBN 9781350257863 (hardback) | ISBN 9781350257870 (paperback) |
ISBN 9781350257887 (epub) | ISBN 9781350257894 (pdf) | ISBN 9781350257900
Subjects: LCSH: WhatsApp (Application software) | Online social networks–Social
aspects–Africa, West. | Online social networks–Political aspects–Africa, West.
Classification: LCC HN820.Z9 I569 2022 (print) | LCC HN820.Z9 (ebook) |
DDC 302.302850966–dc23/eng/20220127
LC record available at https://lccn.loc.gov/2022003854
LC ebook record available at https://lccn.loc.gov/2022003855

ISBN:	HB:	978-1-3502-5786-3
	PB:	978-1-3502-5787-0
	ePDF:	978-1-3502-5789-4
	eBook:	978-1-3502-5788-7

Typeset by Integra Software Services Pvt. Ltd.
Printed and bound in Great Britain

To find out more about our authors and books visit www.bloomsbury.com
and sign up for our newsletters.

Contents

Figure and Tables

Figure

Tables

List of contributors

Na'ima Hafiz Abubakar, Bayero University, Nigeria.

Fortune Afatakpa, Dominion University, Nigeria.

Simon Allison, *The Continent*, South Africa.

Sarah Burris, University of Toronto, Canada.

Lynn Cockburn, University of Toronto, Canada.

Nwachukwu Egbunike, Pan Atlantic University, Lagos.

Patrick Egwu, University of Witwatersrand, South Africa.

Elena Gadjanova, University of Exeter, UK.

Idayat Hassan, Centre for Democracy and Development, Nigeria.

Jamie Hitchen, independent researcher and Honorary Research Fellow at the University of Birmingham, UK.

Feyisitan Ijimakinwa, University of Ibadan, Nigeria.

Sait Matty Jaw, University of The Gambia.

Gabrielle Lynch, University of Warwick, UK.

Louis Mbibeh, University of Bamenda, Cameroon.

Anya Nadege, independent researcher, Cameroon.

Julius Nganji, University of Toronto, Canada

Temitayo Olofinlua, independent researcher, Nigeria.

Kamila Pacholek, University of Toronto, Canada.

Madalina Prostean, University of Toronto, Canada.

Ghadafi Saibu, PhD Candidate at the University of Bayreuth, Germany.

Kolawole Talabi, independent media practitioner, Italy.

Acknowledgements

We are deeply indebted to the knowledge and insights provided by the authors in this volume who have worked tirelessly with us on their chapters.

Particular mention is due for Elena Gadjanova and her co-authors, whose forthcoming work on the application of the notion of 'pavement radio' to the spread of information of WhatsApp, inspired our discussion of the idea in the introduction to this volume.

We also wish to place on record our gratitude for the ongoing support that the Open Society Foundation in West Africa has provided to the Centre for Democracy and Development to work on improving the understanding of digital life and interactions across West Africa in the past five years.

Special thanks to Su Muhereza and Maggie Dwyer for their invaluable feedback on the introduction that only further strengthened the arguments it makes.

Introduction: A new platform for old networks? WhatsApp and everyday life in West Africa

Idayat Hassan and Jamie Hitchen

Since its launch in 2009, WhatsApp has acquired more than two billion users worldwide, with more than half of those coming after 2014, the year it was acquired by Facebook for US$19 billion.[1] Facebook has since evolved into Meta. Bringing together its applications and technologies under one company brand, illustrates the company's apparent desire to make the metaverse, *the* internet. But in as many as thirty African countries Facebook has been the internet for many people coming online for the first time, as a result of the company's 'Free Basics' programme. In short, 'it provides mobile users with access to a small number of data-lite websites of basic services, free of data charge – a model widely described as a *walled-garden* internet experience.'[2] It was banned in India in 2015 after a legal challenge successfully argued that it was in violation of net neutrality principles given that the Free Basics model gave Facebook powers to act as an internet gatekeeper by deciding what services would be made available.[3]

Facebook's motivation for trying to add millions of new users to its platform from untapped markets is driven by economic imperatives. Collecting data provided by its users and selling it to advertisers is fundamental to how the company operates. With Africa's population continuing to grow rapidly, and coming online at a similar rate, efforts

Idayat Hassan is Director of the Centre for Democracy and Development, Abuja.
Jamie Hitchen is an independent researcher and an Honorary Research Fellow at the University of Birmingham.

to promote access to its platform across the continent – as was the ambition of Free Basics and the building of underwater cables to better connect select countries on the continent to the internet[4] – have been seen as acts of 'digital colonialism'.[5] And with data protection and data privacy laws weak, poorly enforced or non-existent in a significant percentage of African contexts,[6] the appropriation of users' data by big tech firms is increasingly viewed as 'data colonialism'.[7] Therefore, it is important to state from the outset that the technology and applications discussed in the subsequent chapters are not neutral. In fact, they are deeply embedded within wider, and global, power structures, that rarely serve African interests. But that does not diminish the fact that they are increasingly integral to everyday life.

WhatsApp in West Africa

WhatsApp is an increasingly influential and ubiquitous in West Africa due to its simple and accessible functions, low data usage and the privacy it offers through its end-to-end encryption of messages. In over 80 per cent of countries in West Africa, WhatsApp is the most downloaded messenger application according to a January 2021 survey.[8] The data shows that whilst the percentage of the population accessing social media remains limited – on average 17.3 per cent of a country's population in West Africa is on social media, with that being as high as 53.7 per cent in Cape Verde and as low as 2.4 per cent in Niger – it is growing significantly. The West Africa region saw a 22 per cent increase in the number of new social media users between January 2020 and January 2021.[9]

WhatsApp is being used to host podcasts that aim to preserve oral history in Senegal,[10] as a platform for interactive drama series in Zimbabwe,[11] to offer banking services in Kenya[12] and to support citizen crowd sourcing of information, on issues such as traffic, in a number of West African cities. In Sierra Leone, the application was used by Freetown City Council to engage with citizen groups through a series of 'digital town halls'. This enabled them to discuss how revenue raised should be spent in their locality in a way that reduced the risk of spreading the Covid-19 virus in 2020.[13] But even for those without direct access to a smartphone or the application, the indirect impact of WhatsApp means that it continues to influence beyond its immediate user base.

Phone-sharing, or gathering around one individual's phone, to listen to voice notes or watch videos is common in many towns and cities across West Africa. Furthermore, WhatsApp users are often influential individuals in the community or society in question and as a result of the ways in which, increasingly, WhatsApp debates and discussions shape and inform traditional media coverage of a whole range of issues, from politics to healthcare, the influence of prominent online voices on the wider information ecosystem is important to consider.

Selnes and Ogeret's 2018 study of three newspapers in Uganda explored how Facebook and Twitter 'serve as alternative channels through which sources with less access to traditional means of communication get their message(s) across to journalists'.[14] In Nigeria, as there are elsewhere on the continent, WhatsApp groups, constituted for journalists and set up by, for example, the armed forces or political parties, provide regular information in the form of press releases and copies of speeches given by prominent officials. Whilst this can help improve the flow of information between institutions and media houses, the fact that this type of content is known to be online makes false content more likely to be believed, if done well, as individuals know that this type of content is already being circulated on WhatsApp. There also remains healthy scepticism of the accuracy of official information in a number of West African contexts. Writing in 2009, Nigerian journalist Sola Odunfa argued that it was more often the case that 'genuine official information is forced out by the rumour mill'.[15] Similar sentiments still prevail across the region.

Ahead of the 2018 general election in Sierra Leone a false story, with images, circulated on WhatsApp that peacekeepers were arriving in the country ahead of polling day – the picture was in fact real, but from the early 2000s when peacekeepers were present in Sierra Leone as its decade-long civil conflict drew to a close – was printed in newspapers and discussed on radio. The level of speculation forced the Inspector General of Police into issuing a statement denying the claims. This is just one example that illustrates the overlap of information flows in the region and the complicated ways in which platforms can influence individuals who are not direct users.

What this means is that the number of WhatsApp downloads, or direct users, is likely to be a significant underestimate of those who access the content indirectly. A WhatsApp audio, which is often conveyed in a local language, can serve the same function as a village radio, in that the information it contains can be broadcast beyond just owners of radios to a much wider audience. From here the information penetrates further into well-established offline rumour networks and becomes the source of what Ellis described as 'pavement radio'[16] discussions.

'Unlike the press, television, or radio, pavement radio is not controlled by any identifiable individual, institution or group of people.'[17] Although there are undoubtedly efforts to shape the topics and direction of discourse given the importance individuals place on the information they hear from it, 'a story cannot be transmitted orally over any considerable distance or for any substantial period unless it is judged to be of interest by a significant number of people.'[18] The importance attached to it comes from the fact that information is communicated by friends, family members or individuals that the listener knows directly and therefore is more likely to trust. The importance of source in assessing the credibility of content is often overlooked but remains vitally important when it comes to validating what is true and what is not.

Ellis's description of 'pavement radio' in the pre-digital era, has many parallels with the way information flows through and on WhatsApp.[19] Information predominantly flows through groups. These are limited to 256 members, although there are ways to increase the numbers beyond that through invitation links. A 2019 survey of 1,000 residents of two Nigerian states – Oyo and Kano – found that

72 per cent of WhatsApp users categorized the average size of a group they are in as being more than fifty persons.[20] But it is not just the size of the groups, but their composition, that is important. They are often centred around pre-existing offline networks and social structures such as extended family, religious affiliations, alumnus connections and professional associations. Transposed online these networks draw on their offline basis to build and strengthen online connections.

Understanding the composition of these groups is important for understanding why and how information – both accurate and false – flows on the application. Whilst social media platforms like Twitter, Facebook and Instagram allow for individuals to engage with others that they do not know personally, WhatsApp offers greater intimacy in that messages are, for the most part, shared directly; either from individuals who are personally known to the users, or through groups in which they will know some, if not all, the members. As Nanjala Nyabola has written in relation to Kenya, but with applicability for elsewhere, 'you can't understand how tech is going to affect a society if you don't understand the society in question. What I think is interesting about misinformation in the political space in Kenya is how it intersects with foregoing patterns of misinformation – how the digital amplifies things that have been happening before.'[21]

Facilitating falsehoods

The intimacy of the platform can partially explain why the circulation of misinformation – information shared without a deliberate intention to mislead – and disinformation – information shared with the deliberate information to mislead – has flourished on WhatsApp. The 'infodemic' which accompanied the Covid-19 pandemic has drawn specific attention to the proliferation of health mis/disinformation on WhatsApp. In 2020, the World Health Organization launched a WhatsApp 'bot' designed to answer questions users might have about the number of cases, symptoms associated with the virus and to counter circulating falsehoods.[22] But the spread of online falsehoods to provide cures for health issues stretches back throughout the last decade. In 2014, when Sierra Leone, Liberia and Guinea experienced an outbreak of Ebola, WhatsApp cures, such as bathing in hot water and/or drinking salt water, circulated online and were acted upon with real-world consequences.

In Nigeria WhatsApp has been a tool for political campaigning since off-cycle gubernatorial elections in 2013 and 2014. But across the region it has become an increasingly integral part of election campaigns in the last five years. In Sierra Leone's 2018 election, efforts to organize formally online were absent, but that did not stop WhatsApp falsehoods spreading about candidates' withdrawals and results that were inaccurate but shaped discourse online and offline.[23] In more recent elections – Nigeria (2019), Ghana (2020) and the Gambia (2021) – a more structured use of WhatsApp has been documented, with important country-specific nuances.[24]

In Nigeria, specifically created vehicles, such as the Buhari Media Centre and Atikultaed Youth Force, that had a loose affiliation to a political party but lacked a direct or formal connection, served as mechanisms for the flow of WhatsApp content that was both aimed at increasing the popularity of their candidate and attacking their opponent.[25] 'We have creative freedom to develop our own stories and narratives' explained one self-styled 'propaganda secretary' in Kano, whilst another argued that 'to a large extent the party doesn't care where the content comes from or whether it is true, only that it helps get them ahead of the opposition.'[26]

In Ghana, social media cyber battalions are formally affiliated with much stronger existing party and political structures. There remains a much higher degree of coordination and control as social media activists are embedded within existing structures rather than having freedom to act as they wish. This, as Saibu et al. discuss in Chapter 1, explains in part why outright falsehoods peddled by these activists are less tolerated in Ghana, than in the Nigerian context. In the Gambia, the overlap between offline and online structures again is to the fore, with parties using the platform to spread audio messages that can be easily taken offline and spread among existing political networks in rural areas.

In all three countries, and elsewhere in the region, WhatsApp groups are the primary way in which messages, created for a specific purpose or goal such as winning political votes, circulate. In addition to more closed groups, where some degree of strategic planning takes place, recipients are either encouraged, or tasked, with spreading content organically into their own personal groups and networks; those which are built around offline social networks. This means that information is not spread directly from groups designed to serve political ends but enters the wider information ecosystem and circulates more organically through pre-existing networks. This is important because the way in which information flows, and the source who shares it, increases the believability of the information to a recipient.

The labelling of a message as having been forwarded many times by WhatsApp in 2019 – and efforts to limit the ability to forward messages to five and then one user at a time – was partially a response to this as it indicates that the sender was not the creator of the message. However, the lack of outreach WhatsApp does to explain its platform changes in West African markets means that this part of the response – which was more broadly designed to slow down the pace at which information could be shared – has not been that effective. The 'forwarded' tag can also be removed by simply copy and pasting text into a new message. Whilst some groups employ 'terms of use', through group administrators, that ban political talk and remove members who fail to adhere to these standards, the vast majority of groups do not police or effectively moderate content and even if they did this it would be very difficult to do regularly given the volume of content that can circulate daily.

Researching WhatsApp

For many residents of West Africa, WhatsApp is a daily port of call for a wide range of information, and even services. Groups are increasingly a key part of the information ecosystem. The chapters aim to provide a clearer idea of how information flows through these structures and how citizens engage with them and the content they enable the sharing of. Understanding this, and the fundamental role it plays in many citizens' lives, can support an improved understanding of the social, economic and political context at large.

The transformative impact of technology is a theme explored in many of the chapters in the book. Whilst not ignoring the negative impacts of false information, not just on politics, the edited collection highlights the ways in which the platform is facilitating conversations and making connections that are taking pre-existing social structures, online. Whilst there is growing literature on its use in facilitating the spread of false information and the role it plays in influencing election processes in the region,[27] there has been little detailed study of the wider, more everyday impacts WhatsApp is having in West Africa in helping to facilitate social organization, enhance economic opportunity and support learning. This is a result of a multitude of factors.

First, there is a global tendency to focus on negative uses of social media and other internet platforms around specific events, rather than on their more positive everyday uses. Second, research funding for understanding the impacts of technology in different contexts remains predominantly focused on technologies impacts on Western contexts. In 2019 WhatsApp awarded twenty grants each of US$50,000 to better understand how misinformation is generated and spread on the application, but only one award supported research in Africa – Nigeria specifically.[28] The fact that the bulk of funding for research is coming from the West is also problematic for researchers looking specifically at WhatsApp given that its importance for political mobilization is very different in the United Kingdom, where it is largely irrelevant, to Nigeria, where it is an integral part of the campaign as Chapter 3 of this volume makes clear. These biases mean that there is a tendency to focus on other social media platforms, particularly Facebook, that have greater resonance in Western countries, even in global funding calls.

Finally for researchers, developing an understanding of how WhatsApp messages circulate and resonate is challenged by the closed and private nature of the application. It would be exceedingly difficult, if not impossible, to track how often a message is shared in order to trace its level of virality, and even if you could, the ethics of doing so remain in question. Then there are the further complications of capturing and deciphering non-text messages, which include memes, videos, pictures and even audios in local languages that are highly context specific, the volume of information that is shared on a daily basis in predominant WhatsApp groups and wider questions about whether this sort of research infringes on the privacy of users.

Understanding the impact of end-to-end encrypted platforms upon public discussions poses a conundrum for researchers that is well articulated by Sehat and Kaminski. 'On the one hand, widely accessible conversations of public importance exist in these spaces, but on the other, the encrypted, private nature of shared messages make the professional ethics of access and collection less than clear.'[29] They highlight four practices that currently prevail: do not enter private chat groups and rely on voluntary contributions; enter specific chat groups with invitation or consent for a publicly identified purpose; enter 'public chat' groups with research identification, allowing for removal or withdrawal when requested; and enter more 'public' private groups but without any identification.[30]

For the most part contributors to this volume relied on voluntary contributions from group members to shape their understanding of unfolding dynamics drawing primarily on qualitative methods. Authors did not enter multiple WhatsApp groups in order to conduct research for this chapter, although some were already members of groups and leveraged this position to shape and enhance their analysis.

This was supported by an understanding that comes from their own use of WhatsApp in the context they are writing about. This is critically important as understandings of socio-cultural and political context are vital to situating narratives or explaining why a seemingly bizarre or mundane story can circulate so widely when others do not. Here Ellis's conception of pavement radio is again illuminating. He notes that 'pavement radio sometimes transmits stories about witchcraft and other phenomena which, to a Western observer, can seem irrational or bizarre. These repay closer study in the light of the imagery of popular culture which retains a foundation in African religion, folklore, and oral history.'[31]

Recent history and lived experience also matter when it comes to interpreting online content. This can partially explain why a rumour that President Buhari had died and been replaced as president of Nigeria by a clone from Sudan named Jubril continued to resonate in 2019 even after it was dismissed as false. Buhari had spent several months of the previous year abroad in hospital, bringing back memories of former president Umaru Yar'Adua, who died in office in 2010 after spending several months abroad being treated for medical ailments. That, coupled with ordinary Nigerian's experience of the healthcare system – that those who are old and sick rarely recover – can explain the continued circulation of the rumour and serves to reiterate the importance of researchers having a wider contextual understanding of the WhatsApp content they are studying, something that this volume has aimed to achieve by working closely with researchers from West Africa.

Outline

The volume opens with three chapters focused on the political uses of WhatsApp drawing on experiences and examples from Ghana, the Gambia and Nigeria. They are followed by two chapters that explore the ways in which WhatsApp can provide a platform for the sale of goods or the acquisition of knowledge in Nigeria and Cameroon respectively. Four further chapters explore how different segments of society in Nigeria – women, the elderly, alumni members and the Catholic church – are using WhatsApp to advance their own agenda or participation. Finally, there is a discussion of how the prevalence and prominence of WhatsApp as a source of information sharing can be used by traditional sources of news to engage more robustly in the digital age.

In Chapter 1, Ghadafi Saibu et al, explore the use of WhatsApp by Ghana's two main political parties – the National Democratic Congress and National Patriotic Party – in rural and urban districts of northern Ghana. They argue that whilst WhatsApp usage is growing significantly in the region between each election, it has not replaced traditional campaign activities. Politics in Ghana remains ground-intensive, and politicians need to remain visible and to display their electoral viability, track record and commitment to constituents to be competitive. Regardless of this, WhatsApp – and other social media platforms as cross-platform information sharing is commonplace – is having a significant impact on campaign messaging in Ghana, albeit in ways that ultimately feed off, and further reinforce, pre-existing structures and strategies.

Ghana's strong, competitive and well-established two leading parties have been able to convert their party structures online, through WhatsApp groups, providing them with quick access to supporters, and ultimately voters. For the most part these groups are used to talk at, rather than with, voters, but intra-party WhatsApp groups are also used to pass information back from the grassroots up, and to discuss and monitor information strategies. The level of control in these formal party groups is quite high, with power vested in administrators, who are often key party officials or members. Campaign content online does not differ significantly to that found offline in that it seeks to affirm the commitment shown by a candidate to his constituency or attack opponents and question their credibility. However, it is interesting to note that party activists on both sides were cautious about creating 'fake news' in these formal channels, fearful that such an approach would lead to citizens viewing their party or candidate as inflammatory.

Chapter 2 situates the use of WhatsApp for political mobilization in a very different political context. The dictatorship of Gambian president Yahya Jammeh came to an end in 2016 after he was voted out of office, twenty-two years on from seizing power. Social media played an important role in uniting and mobilizing an opposition coalition to do so. Sait Matty Jaw looks at the specific role that WhatsApp played, not just in mobilizing and forging consensus ahead of the December 2016 poll but how various WhatsApp groups, that eventually culminated in the 'Democratic Gambia' group, created a platform for dialogue and political debate particularly between activists in the Gambia and diaspora members living outside the country as to how best to challenge Jammeh.

Tensions between a more confrontational approach, often supported by those outside of the country, and more strategic efforts proposed by in-country activists were reflected online. But the ongoing space for dialogue created on WhatsApp eventually enabled a consensus and played a key role in ousting Jammeh by linking the two groups of activists. During the election campaign period, WhatsApp groups enabled diaspora political organizers and in-country allies to work together to ensure the opposition coalition messages reached sympathetic ears. This digital outreach significantly helped the ground game of the coalition by creating a networked space, to an extent, free of state oversight, where they could operate. However, as Jaw notes the nature of these groups is always evolving, meaning that they splinter frequently. This happened in the Gambia both as disagreements emerged as to how best to fight back against the Jammeh regime, and then again after his ouster. With the purpose of the WhatsApp group achieved, efforts to reorient it to focus on how best to support the development of democracy have been disrupted by divergent political views among coalition supporters.

In Chapter 3, the role of WhatsApp in Nigeria's recent political campaigns is analysed by Nwachukwu Egbunike. Drawing on insights from campaign managers it unpicks the ways in which WhatsApp can support election bids by allowing for more targeted messaging of prospective voters and by enabling attacks on political opponents. Groups are a key part of the dissemination of information with 'a sophisticated campaign broadcast chain... the norm in Nigerian elections' for individual candidates and parties.

But whilst WhatsApp is seen as a crucial part of the social media campaign in Nigeria, Egbunike is keen not to overstress its importance noting that the role played by godfathers in the selection of candidates, the prevalence of vote buying and even the credibility of some polls themselves means that there is a limit to the impact that digital campaigns can have in the Nigerian context. He argues that WhatsApp has been growing in importance for political campaigning since 2015 in Nigeria, and will continue to be an important tool, but that it is yet to really transform the status quo in a significant way.

In Chapter 4, Kolawole Talabi highlights how WhatsApp is used by small business owners in southwest Nigeria to advertise, market and even sell products to clients across the country and beyond. Using the experience of tailors, the chapter highlights the ways in which WhatsApp is increasingly becoming a marketplace in which users take advantage of features of the application, such as the status function, to advertise new products, primarily to existing clients – with the client based expanded through word of mouth and the cross-posting of information across social media channels. Whilst online shopping facilitated by WhatsApp may make the overall process much smoother, there are still offline roadblocks to navigate such as how to deliver products and the looming threat of internet or platform shutdowns.

But WhatsApp networks and groups are not just marketing tools. They are also used as support mechanisms for small enterprise owners working in a similar sector, in a way akin, but different, to an unofficial union. The Christian Designers Hub is one such example. Members pay a fee to join and are added to WhatsApp groups where they can discuss challenges and share and receive tips and advice from other members. These sorts of networks are not necessarily new, but they are much easier to maintain and sustain online and so WhatsApp has been a key enabler of their growth and success. This is also true of efforts, documented in this chapter, to use the platform to provide skills training in tailoring at a fraction of the cost that would be required to attend more formal education facilities.

WhatsApp as a space and tool for learning is explored in depth in Chapter 5, which looks at how the application was used to create a group that brought together forty diverse individuals, mostly from Cameroon, to support knowledge sharing and skills acquisition in mental health and trauma-informed care. Despite the challenges of ongoing conflict, and regular internet shutdowns, the WhatsApp group was able to serve as a valuable resource for healthcare professionals working in these challenging circumstances. Members not only found the opportunities for peer learning to be one of its benefits, but also benefited from the shared sense of community important given the difficult and challenging nature of the work and the context.

The chapter argues that from this experience WhatsApp has the potential to be an effective platform to host a virtual community of practice given that most users are already well versed in its basic functions and the fact that it allows for the sharing of audio, videos and documents in a setting that is less formal but one that supports feedback and interaction. In short, it illustrates how WhatsApp can offer a platform for enabling diverse and dispersed professionals to interact in meaningful ways, overcoming barriers imposed by time, location and context.

Nigeria's elderly population have regularly been depicted as key enablers of the spread of falsehoods,[32] but Chapter 6 looks to provide a more nuanced look at how older users interact on WhatsApp. Temitayo Olofinlua explores how predominantly retired, Nigerians in the southwest of the country are keeping in touch and even building new connections and networks that can keep them more informed and connected using the application. It highlights how WhatsApp has become quickly embedded into everyday rituals and argues that it is not creating new networks and friendships but strengthening and reaffirming existing ones.

By way of conclusion, it draws attention to how the elderly are 'learning as they go' when it comes to developing their skills online. It argues that rather than blaming them for the spread of falsehoods, there should be more concerted efforts targeting older users, so that they can be empowered to reduce the spread of falsehoods and better inform themselves when it comes to sharing information on WhatsApp, something all admitted to doing regularly.

In Chapter 7, Feyisitan Ijimakinwa and Fortune Afatakpa seek to highlight the ways in which WhatsApp groups – in this example centred around being an alumni of the Christlove Fellowship – can provide multiple societal benefits for members in a replication and extension of offline networks. They start by tracing the evolution of the fellowship and its movement online, and then to WhatsApp, as a way of members staying in better contact. It then highlights the multiple ways in which members – drawn from Nigeria and beyond – gain benefits from being part of the group. This includes the way in which the network is used to circulate job offers and to provide connections to individuals looking for healthcare advice or even remote treatment.

During the Covid-19 lockdown, the chapter details how the alumni leadership organized WhatsApp webinars where leading financial experts offered advice on how best to mitigate the economic challenges posed by a government imposed lockdown. Drawing on the work of Omanga[33] it highlights how these 'digital publics' are creating new spaces for engagement. Although the chapter focuses on just one set of alumni WhatsApp groups, it can potentially offer insights into the ways in which other community or professional associations are utilizing WhatsApp networks to support and engage members in similar ways in Nigeria and beyond.

In Chapter 8, Patrick Egwu seeks to understand how the Catholic Church in Nigeria is looking to utilize social media platforms and private messenger applications like WhatsApp to spread the gospel to a new, and younger, audience. In highlighting the way in which more and more of the content of priests is being shared with online audiences, and how more material is being generated with an online audience in mind, Egwu shows how the Catholic Church are looking to become more of a daily feature in everyday life, rather than a peripheral once-a-week presence. This has only been accentuated during the Covid-19 pandemic, which limited the size of congregations significantly.

The chapter also highlights how WhatsApp is being used by the sisterhood of the church to coordinate activities aimed at alleviating poverty or to tackle wider societal challenges. Here they rely on internal communication to strengthen their advocacy and engagement efforts. Just like in other chapters in the volume it highlights how WhatsApp is not radically overhauling existing structures of practices but providing more efficient ways of communicating that, in the case of the church, can improve both its internal functions and its external proselytizing efforts.

Women in Kano, a state in northern Nigeria, are finding a greater political voice, and space, online as Na'ima Hafiz Abubakar shows in Chapter 9. Historically a significant percentage of women's engagement in electoral politics, and conversations about it, in conservative northern Nigeria have been determined by male household heads, but with the growth of WhatsApp they are finding ways to engage in politics both around elections and in the periods in between. First, the application is enabling women to access greater unfiltered political information. This can be both articles and analysis pieces but also through the relaying of campaign rallies in video, audio and picture form that women would normally have to challenge cultural norms to attend. Now they can hear what prospective candidates have to say from their own home, and even more discuss these ideas with other women in WhatsApp groups that they are part of. These women-only spaces were preferred by many of the individuals interviewed and helped to create a sense of online community that draws on some degree of shared experience.

In recognition of this Nigeria's two main political parties, the All Progressives Congress and People's Democratic Party have encouraged their local female mobilizers to create WhatsApp groups of influential women in their communities or local government area, where they can both engage with them about what a candidate aspires to do, or is doing, when in office. These groups can also be used by women to communicate with the elected official when in office when they are failing to deliver on promises outline during campaigns. The chapter also highlights examples of how government ministries in the state are using the platform to serve similar goals when it comes to the rollout of initiatives targeting women. It argues that when used in this way WhatsApp can be supportive and foster more accountability and responsive governance, though it acknowledges that this must compete with the challenges that come from misinformation and disinformation.

Overall, the focus of this edited volume is less about the threat of fake news, though it is undoubtedly important, and more about some of the ways the increased information flows are impacting on everyday life. But one part of everyday life is how individuals consume and absorb news and one way that organizations and media are fighting back against fake news is by getting on the platform and creating better quality of information. The final chapter reflects on the experience of *The Continent*, Africa's first weekly WhatsApp newspaper.

Discussing the challenge of being a journalist during the Covid-19 infodemic, editor of *The Continent*, and chapter author, Simon Allison describes it like 'standing on the dance floor of a crowded nightclub. The music is blaring, the strobe lights are flashing, there are fire alarms going off in the background and everyone is shouting different things in your direction. And somehow, you have to make your own voice heard above the cacophony.' Allison decided that WhatsApp could provide the platform and *The Continent* was born. The chapter highlights how they took inspiration from similar initiatives in Zimbabwe to produce a 'PDF Newspaper' for the digital age. *The Continent* is an effort to use the very same channels and organic sharing methods – subscribers are encouraged to share not widely but with close friends and family – used to spread falsehoods to promote credible and accurate writing and analysis about Africa. It is an attempts to bring the news to an application that increasing numbers of Africans are using as their primary source of information are explored in detail.

Throughout all ten chapters in this edited volume, the authors illustrate the ways in which WhatsApp is becoming increasing influential in everyday life in West Africa. They document how it is not creating or reinventing ways that people access information, stay in touch, organize around politics, buy goods or even learn, but building on, and gradually redefining, existing structures and networks. This is not a WhatsApp revolution, but an evolution. One that is impacting across societies and across sectors and one that is likely to grow even more significant in the next decade as more and more West Africans come online.

Notes

1   Parmy Olson. 2014. 'Facebook closes $19 billion WhatsApp deal'. *Forbes Magazine*. 6 October. Available at https://www.forbes.com/sites/parmyolson/2014/10/06/facebook-closes-19-billion-whatsapp-deal/?sh=311a9f8c5c66

2   Toussaint Nothias. 'Access granted: Free basics in Africa'. *Media, Culture and Society* 42, 3 (2020), p. 330.

3   Nothias, 'Access granted', pp. 329–48.

4   Ryan Browne. 2020. 'Facebook is building a huge undersea cable around Africa to boost internet access in the continent'. *CNBC*. 14 May. Available at https://www.cnbc.com/2020/05/14/facebook-building-undersea-cable-in-africa-to-boost-internet-access.html

5   Michael Kwet. 2019. 'Digital colonialism is threatening the Global South'. *Al Jazeera*. 13 March. Available at https://www.aljazeera.com/opinions/2019/3/13/digital-colonialism-is-threatening-the-global-south

6   Privacy International. 2020. '2020 is a crucial year to fight for data protection in Africa'. 3 March. Available at https://privacyinternational.org/long-read/3390/2020-crucial-year-fight-data-protection-africa

7   Nima Elmi. 2020. 'Is Big Tech setting Africa back?' *Foreign Policy*. 11 November. Available at https://foreignpolicy.com/2020/11/11/is-big-tech-setting-africa-back/

8   Simon Kemp. 2021. 'Digital 2021: Global overview report'. *Data Reportal*. Available at https://datareportal.com/reports/digital-2021-global-overview-report

9   Kemp, 'Digital 2021'.

10 Nellie Peyton. 2021. 'Senegal is preserving its oral history in a podcast'. *Quartz Africa*. 31 May. Available at https://qz.com/africa/2014810/senegal-preserves-oral-history-in-a-podcast-with-massamba-gueye/

11 Nyasha Bhobo. 2021. 'A look at Zimbabwe's first WhatsApp drama series'.
    iAfrikan. 3 June. Available at https://iafrikan.com/2021/06/03/zimbabwes-
    first-whatsapp-drama-series/

12 Victor Amadala. 2021. 'Absa Bank Kenya launches WhatsApp banking'.
    The Star. 10 August. Available at https://www.the-star.co.ke/business/
    kenya/2021-08-10-absa-bank-kenya-launches-whatsapp-banking/

13 Freetown City Council. 2020. *Press Release: FCC to Start Digital Town
    Hall Initiative.*

14 Kristin Orgeret and Florence Selnes. 'Social media in Uganda:
    Revitalising news journalism?' *Media, Culture and Society* 42, 3 (2020),
    pp. 380–97.

15 Sola Odunfa. 2009. 'Lies, politics and Nigeria's great rumour mill'.
    BBC News. 2 December. Available at http://news.bbc.co.uk/2/hi/
    africa/8389020.stm

16 Stephen Ellis. 'Tuning in to pavement radio'. *African Affairs* 88, 352
    (1989), pp. 321–30.

17 Ellis, 'Pavement radio'. p. 321.

18 Ibid.

19 See Elena Gadjanova, Gabrielle Lynch and Ghadafi Saibu. 'Pavement
    radio in the social media age: How misinformation crosses digital divides
    in northern Ghana'. Unpublished Working Paper

20 Survey conducted by the University of Birmingham and Centre for
    Democracy and Development. Unpublished.

21 Catherine Tsalikis. 2019. 'Nanjala Nyabola on the "digital colonialism"
    transforming Kenya's political discourse'. *Centre for International
    Governance Innovation.* 5 November. Available at https://www.cigionline.
    org/articles/nanjala-nyabola-digital-colonialism-transforming-kenyas-
    political-discourse/

22 Shawn Farai. 2020. 'WHO adopts WhatsApp platform developed in South
    Africa to provide information on the coronavirus outbreak'. *Business
    and Human Rights Resource Centre.* 27 March. Available at https://
    www.business-humanrights.org/en/latest-news/who-adopts-whatsapp-
    platform-developed-in-south-africa-to-provide-information-on-the-
    coronavirus-outbreak/

23 Maggie Dwyer et al. 2019. 'Between excitement and skepticism: The role
    of WhatsApp in Sierra Leone's 2018 election'. in Maggie Dwyer and Tom

Molony (eds), *Social Media and Politics in Africa: Democracy, Censorship and Security.* Zed Books Ltd, 2019, pp. 105–28.

24 See Idayat Hassan et al. 2019. 'WhatsApp and Nigeria's 2019 election: Mobilising the people, protecting the vote'. *Centre for Democracy and Development,* July; Elena Gadjanova at al. 2019. 'Social Media, Cyber Battalions and Political Mobilisation in Ghana'. *University of Exeter.* November; and Idayat Hassan and Jamie Hitchen. 2020. 'Forums of debate? WhatsApp and the Gambia's political transition'. *Centre for Democracy and Development.* April.

25 Hassan et al. 'WhatsApp and Nigeria's 2019 election'.

26 Idayat Hassan and Jamie Hitchen. 2019. 'Nigeria's propaganda secretaries'. *Mail and Guardian.* 18 April. Available at https://mg.co.za/article/2019-04-18-00-nigerias-propaganda-secretaries/

27 See for example Dwyer et al. 'Between excitement and skepticism': Nic Cheeseman, Jonathan Fisher, Idayat Hassan and Jamie Hitchen. 'Social media disruption: Nigeria's WhatsApp politics'. *Journal of Democracy* 31, 3 (2020), pp. 145–59.

28 WhatsApp Misinformation Award Announcement. Available at https://www.whatsapp.com/research/awards/announcement/

29 Connie Moon Sehat and Aleksi Kaminski. 2020. 'Considerations for closed messaging research in democratic contexts'. *The Carter Centre.* September. p. 1.

30 Ibid.

31 Ellis, 'Pavement radio', p. 327.

32 See for example Adaoba Tricia Nwaubani. 2020. 'Letter from Africa: Why Nigerians are muting their mothers on WhatsApp'. *BBC News.* 8 June. https://www.bbc.com/news/world-africa-52927678

33 Duncan Omanga. 'WhatsApp as digital publics: The *Nakuru Analysts* and the evolution of participation in county governance in Kenya'. *Journal of Eastern African Studies* 13, 1 (2019), pp. 175–91.

1

WhatsApp and political messaging at the periphery: Insights from northern Ghana

Gabrielle Lynch, Ghadafi Saibu and Elena Gadjanova

With relatively cheap smartphones available across the country; time-limited data bundles and schemes such as Facebook's Free Basics (which provide unlimited or free access to various social media platforms);[1] 'cultural values of sociality, interconnectedness, interdependence and conviviality';[2] and a widespread popular interest in current affairs,[3] it is unsurprising that an increasing number of Ghanaians are active social media users.[4] This includes the country's political aspirants and party activists who – in an extremely competitive electoral system that sees regular transfers of power between the National Democratic Congress (NDC) and New Patriotic Party (NPP) – are always looking for a competitive edge. In 2016, the NPP seemed to gain this edge, at least in part, through their more effective use of social media. As the incumbent president and NDC flagbearer, John Mahama, lamented in the wake of his defeat:

> Social media was coming into its own... and the NPP used it very effectively to really create the perception – exaggerated – of our administration that the economy was in a big mess.[5]

Or as one NPP official claimed, 'we used [social media] extensively [in 2016] and it contributed about 40 per cent to our victory.'[6] This common

Gabrielle Lynch is Professor of Comparative Politics at the University of Warwick. Ghadafi Saibu is Junior Fellow at the Bayreuth International Graduate School of African Studies and a PhD Candidate at the University of Bayreuth, Germany. Elena Gadjanova is Assistant Professor in Politics at the University of Exeter.

evaluation led both parties to invest even more heavily in social media ahead of the country's 2020 elections.

But how is this increased use of social media helping to shape electoral campaigns and party politics? It is evident from recent studies that social media has not replaced traditional campaign activities: politics in Ghana remains ground-intensive and politicians need to remain visible and to display their electoral viability, track record, and commitment to constituents to be competitive.[7] In this context, an investment in social media constitutes additional work that enables candidates and parties to conduct limited fund-raising, to better organize their activities – from the scheduling of rallies to voter registration drives and monitoring of polling stations, to sharing messages and propaganda with potential voters; and to strategize on, and manage, their campaign messages and propaganda through intra-party groups.[8] In this chapter, we focus not only on the sharing of messages with voters but also on the organization and control of campaign messaging by parties. The latter is an issue that has received relatively little attention despite widespread concern with 'fake news' and the fact that (dis)information campaigns in other contexts have often involved surprisingly 'professionalised and institutionalised work structures'.[9]

The chapter draws upon primary research conducted in 2019, and focuses in particular on the use of WhatsApp by NPP and NDC officials in four constituencies in northern Ghana – Tamale Central, Tamale North, Tamale South, and Nanton (see Figure 1). In terms of primary research, we conducted sixty-five qualitative interviews and eight focus group discussions (FGDs) with politicians, campaign strategists, political communicators, political activists, youth group members, journalists and civil society workers between February and July 2019 in Ghana's capital city, Accra, and in and around Tamale in northern Ghana as part of a larger project on social media and political mobilization in the 2016 and 2020 elections. We also designed a survey, which IPSOS-Ghana then conducted with a representative sample of 1,600 respondents across the four constituencies in July 2019.

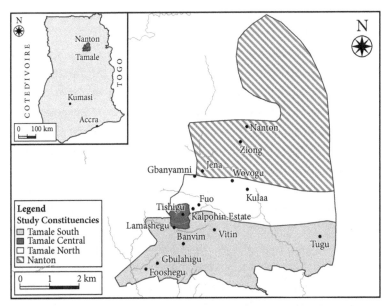

Figure 1 The four study constituencies in northern Ghana. Compiled by Issahaka Fuseini.

Tamale and its environs were selected for several reasons. First, as an area in which both the NPP and NDC secure national seats[10] and a significant share of the presidential vote,[11] the setting allowed us to look at how social media is used by the dominant parties in a competitive environment. Second, as an area that has historically been socio-economically and politically marginal, and which is physically far from Accra, it allowed us to look at how party messaging spreads from the political centre to the periphery. Finally, as an area that includes both the country's third largest city and remote and relatively poor rural areas, it allowed us to look – within a relatively small geographic area – at how social media is used to disseminate, but also discuss, organize, and control messages in areas where a majority of the local population are regular and direct social media users (as in Tamale municipality), as well as in areas where only a minority are (as in rural Nanton). Our focus in this chapter is thus on messaging at the periphery, rather than at the national level or political centre.[12]

WhatsApp, unlike largely open platforms such as Facebook and Twitter, is particularly well suited for intra-party organization and mass mobilization. As a closed platform that allows for encrypted conversations within administrated groups of up to 256 people – and in a context largely free of reports of spyware hacking of the platform – WhatsApp is the preferred media for intra-party organization and discussion. At the same time, WhatsApp's functionality, which allows people to share and forward texts, voice recordings, memes and weblinks – as well as users' ability to easily access messages whenever they go online – means that it is now a more popular communication application than Facebook or other social media platforms.[13] Not only is WhatsApp popular, but it is common for Ghanaians to belong to multiple (often large) WhatsApp groups, which means that, even at the periphery, activists and candidates can discuss, strategize and organize within intra-party groups, and then use their membership of other groups to disseminate messages. Those messages are then also shared – by activists and supporters alike – across various social media platforms and offline.

This chapter starts with a brief overview of the structures that parties and candidates have developed to organize their messaging via WhatsApp before turning to how messaging is managed in practice and with what impact in terms of the types of (mis)information disseminated. What we find is that the institutionalized and highly competitive nature of Ghana's political parties, and the heavy reliance of ordinary citizens on politicized networks for access to jobs and other opportunities, have facilitated an impressive social media communications structure – with WhatsApp used to connect NPP and NDC party leaders and office holders in Accra with those at the regional, constituency and ward levels, even in the most remote and rural parts of the country. This structure is then paralleled and reinforced by local-level networks established by incumbent and aspirant MPs and assembly members, and by more informal networks. These structures allow for the incredibly quick and efficient relay of information; group members are also used to discuss party and candidate messaging in ways that allow for both top-down directives and bottom-up input. We find that this messaging is then monitored by group administrators and prominent members in ways that encourage communicators to stick to a party-line. This line includes both positive campaigns and 'decampaigns', or efforts to persuade voters to reject alternative candidates; but simultaneously discourages disinformation that could be easily debunked or might otherwise put off potential or existing supporters, such as content likely to increase ethnic divisions or incite violence. In Ghana this helps to moderate some of social media's more divisive and polarizing tendencies. In short, WhatsApp is having a significant impact on campaign messaging in Ghana, but in ways that ultimately feed off, and further reinforce, pre-existing structures and strategies.

Party machines and cyber battalions

Ghana's politics is dominated by the NPP and NDC: the two secured every parliamentary seat in 2016, all but one in 2020, and over 98 per cent of the presidential vote in both elections. The NDC and NPP are popularly associated with distinct ideological visions, connected to the parties' Nkrumahist or Danquah/Busia roots. The NPP self-identifies, and is widely associated, with an intellectual, business and professional elite dedicated to liberal governance and a market economy; and the NDC with social democratic appeals and more rural and marginalized communities. With time this distinction has become increasingly blurred with both parties offering increasingly similar manifesto pledges as they move to the middle of the political spectrum.[14] This has gone hand-in-hand with both parties making inroads into each other's support bases as is evident in northern Ghana where the NDC was initially dominant, but where the NPP now regularly wins parliamentary seats and a significant proportion of the presidential vote.[15]

The inroads that both parties have made into each other's strongholds are further evidenced in the development of sophisticated and extensive party structures that connect the political centre with regional, constituency and ward committees across the country. These structures are reinforced by individual candidate networks and by more informal groups of supporters, such as those who gather at party-branded 'sheds'.[16] This impressive level of activity and reach is rendered possible by strong socialized attachments with particular parties (through family, friends and clubs), cross-ethnic campaigns and regular transfers of power, while many also hope to gain from their activism via immediate handouts or future socio-economic and political opportunities.[17]

By 2019, both the NPP and NDC had integrated WhatsApp into these formal structures and informal networks. This included the appointment or election of communications officers at every level of the party structure; with those officials then connected with each other through intra-party WhatsApp groups. As one NPP member explained:

> The regional national communication director he has programmed a WhatsApp group. So, that the various regional communication directors are part of that particular WhatsApp group. When there is information or when the party has come up with some certain offer of information, the national communication director has to put it on that platform. The various regional directors will then put it in their various regional communication platform ... [and] their constituency communication team ... [and] the electoral area communicators will then copy the message and send to various electoral areas. That's how the message is being channelled.[18]

These party structures were paralleled and reinforced by those established by aspirant and incumbent politicians, and by an 'army' of social media communicators. The latter included those on allowances, of as little as GH₵20 (US$3.50) a week for data, who were key members of intra-party and candidate WhatsApp groups, as well as those who hoped to come to the attention of party officials and candidates through their public activism and – in so doing – either be recruited as a paid online communicator themselves or to benefit in some other way in the short- to medium-term.[19] Moreover, while many of these aspirant communicators were linked to intra-party or candidate WhatsApp groups only indirectly through friends and associates, others were already members having been recognized by group administrators as active supporters.

Finally, there were ordinary supporters and party members who – for various reasons – often engaged in political mobilization of their own. As one interviewee explained of an NDC parliamentary candidate's campaign in 2016:

> We had a group, [an] old students association group, and he found a way of getting into that group on WhatsApp. And then he was able to tell us his aims and what he would do for our communities should he be given the vote. And through that we, those who were in the communities with our people … we were doing the campaign for him.[20]

These formal party and candidate structures and informal networks pervaded across northern Ghana, extending into the poorest neighbourhoods and remotest villages. Intra-party and candidate WhatsApp group members were then proactive in sharing party messages both online and offline.

First, WhatsApp messages relayed via intra-party or candidate groups were forwarded through the multiple WhatsApp groups that characterize everyday Ghanaian life. As one interviewee explained:

> In this country usually you have WhatsApp groups. In every constituency you'll have WhatsApp groups that have more women in … like a market women's group … Some that will be more youth maybe like a motor bike taxi association; some that will be more students [like] some university platform; or some that will be older, maybe a teacher's group.[21]

Party officials and activists proactively sought to join these groups so as to use their membership to share campaign messages and propaganda: 'You find a lot of people using WhatsApp. They have WhatsApp groups. One message is sent out and then it's copied over, and sent all across. Before you know it, a lot of the groups have that information.'[22] These messages were shared in various forms – including text, memes, voice notes and videos – and languages, depending on the message and target group.

Second, messages received on WhatsApp were regularly shared through social media platforms such as Facebook and Twitter with attention given to the comparative advantages of each platform. As one interviewee explained, 'Facebook allows you to go back and edit. WhatsApp doesn't.' As a result, long write-ups are on Facebook, while 'short clip messages are on WhatsApp because … you can read it before and then you send it'.[23]

Third, intra-party and candidate WhatsApp groups helped to inform traditional media content: as journalists and presenters used social media to source and fact-check stories,[24] and as group members appeared on, or phoned into, increasingly ubiquitous radio talk shows.[25] This dissemination was encouraged by parties and candidates. National party communicators, for example, prepared 'speaking points', which they then shared 'among a group of communicators across the entire country', such that, if a member 'appear[ed] on radio, these are the issues that you are speaking on'.[26]

Finally, intra-party WhatsApp messages were shared by politicians, activists and supporters through the rallies, door-to-door canvassing, and community events (such as funerals and school meetings) that characterize Ghana's extended campaigns,[27] and through 'pavement radio'. As group members discussed WhatsApp conversations through the 'popular and unofficial discussion of current affairs' in marketplaces, places of worship, bars and the like.[28] These offline communications were critical as it meant that messages initially shared via intra-party and candidate WhatsApp groups were systematically passed on to ordinary citizens including those without direct social media access.

The number of people involved in this dissemination of information was rendered possible – and further reinforced – by already well-established party structures. As a result, it was perhaps unsurprising that smaller political parties were unable to compete with the well-oiled NPP and NDC machines.

> The limited resources of the smaller opposition parties mean that they cannot invest in communications teams or 'social media armies' to the same extent, nor can they generate the same level of voluntary engagement through digital entrepreneurs … [as a result] the messages of the smaller parties get drowned out by the large and increasingly well-organised social media machines and the armies of hopeful volunteers of the big two.[29]

The way that WhatsApp was used by political parties and candidates to relay information down a chain of command into all walks of life was striking. However, just as striking, was the extent to which WhatsApp was being used to discuss, strategize, monitor and control messaging.

Discussing, and holding, the party line

In Ghana's 2020 election, WhatsApp and social media platforms were largely used to share information, rather than to engage in more interactive discussions.[30] This finding is in keeping with studies in other contexts that have found that citizens are largely 'campaigned *at*, but not *with*'; with online efforts tending 'to avoid the full interactive affordances of digital media'.[31] Yet, this does not mean that information was pre-determined or that it flowed in only one direction. On the contrary, intra-party WhatsApp groups were used to pass information not only down or across, but also up, and to discuss and monitor information strategies.

The channelling of information from the bottom-up was recognized as important as it helped to ensure that officials and candidates were aware of pertinent talking points that would resonate with different groups and communities. As one NPP communicator explained:

> We are with the community. we know what is going on there about the economy. So, we also give them [our national leaders] information about the current situation on the ground.[32]

Such feedback was encouraged by party leaders and strategists, and could be almost instantaneous:

> Most of them [the party leaders], they usually give us 'oh tomorrow by this time I will be on radio station. This are the topics that we will be going through.' We will also bring our ideas, and on the groups so that we also share it … as the panel are seated … we also sometimes give them ideas by WhatsApp. The host may throw up some question whereby … you will have a better idea of it than the panellist, then you also just WhatsApp him the answer.[33]

Yet more striking still was the amount of discussion within these intra-party and candidate groups about the campaign line. As one NDC communicator explained:

> We have political groups on WhatsApp where we meet together to have internal political discussions among ourselves before we come out to engage in debate with our political opponents.[34]

An NPP communicator confirmed how,

> we collectively examine the post together, if there is nothing wrong with it, it is approved for public sharing, but if there is a problem it is either edited or dropped.[35]

Not only were party messages discussed via these intra-party WhatsApp groups, but these groups – often through the group administrator – were used to monitor and manage the same:

> Each and every WhatsApp group you have an administrator or someone who manage[s] the WhatsApp group. Who direct[s] you what to do and what not to do.[36]

This oversight was impressive in its efficiency and reach. As one constituency-level NPP communications officer explained in rural Nanton:

> When you write something, it goes through the constituency director before it [is] posted … If the constituency communication director assesses it and sees it [is] not suitable to go public he will advise that it should be dropped. And even if he doesn't see it before you post it,

some members of the regional communications team might still see it. They will inform him that 'we have seen this post from a member of your team in the constituency, so work on it'. He will then call you and talk to you about it. When you talk, it is possible you might delete the post or edit it … Even if a party member who is not in the communication team … posts something about the party which is not suitable to be on social media, and the regional or the national teams see it, the communication directors will try to locate the person to verify the authenticity, and to advise the person on either to delete or edit it. So, it is the constituency, regional and the national directors who monitor social media for the political parties in our politics.[37]

The same was true for the NDC:

When a member says something, which is overboard, he [the communications director] will draw your attention to it and advise you how to put it better next time. These regulations are on all the platforms. Everything that goes on the platform he is aware of it.[38]

Interestingly, both parties sought to use this oversight to encourage creative messaging that was more likely to resonate with particular groups and areas. As one NDC communicator explained:

We have a WhatsApp group for ourselves where we all meet and discuss issues … that one is restricted … [however] because we usually don't want the information to look contrived, like it has been deliberately said … [we say] you go out there, you use own words, you use your own strategy, the best strategy you think can reach your audience well … once you get the central idea about what you are doing, you can in any way project it, as far as it arrives at the same thing.[39]

This approach encouraged creativity – from ensuring that critiques appeared to come from ordinary citizens so that they looked 'simply socially critical' rather than overtly partisan[40] to discussions about the pictures most likely to give a story 'more traction',[41] and use of different formats (texts, memes, recorded voice notes) and language.

Not only were these groups highly strategic in their approach, but sanctions were imposed on those who transgressed the rules or shared information deemed to be damaging to the party or candidate's efforts. As one party activist explained:

> There are rules that you need to go by, so if we find out that [someone has broken those rules], we normally issue a warning to them before exiting them. I personally sometime call them, 'ohh, this person, what you are putting on the platform is not acceptable so you better stop or avoid it'.[42]

With sanctions also used against those who were regarded as insufficiently loyal, or as a potential 'spy' for another political party or candidate. This oversight even extended into the more rural and remote areas of Nanton:

> There are always rules and regulations governing the group. So, there are sanctions for those who violate the rules. Some of the sanctions are either the person is temporarily or permanently banned from the group. If it is WhatsApp for example, he is [sometimes] excluded from the group for some months, weeks before he is reconnected to the group.[43]

This level of organization and oversight is significant in and of itself, but it also meant that campaign messaging by party officials, social media 'armies', and ordinary supporters were more controlled than they might at first appear, with important implications for the type of messaging that was both encouraged and sanctioned.

WhatsApp and the messaging dis/encouraged

In multiparty Ghana, campaign messaging has tended to focus on persuading voters that a particular candidate and party is viable, that they are generous and able to assist, and that they are well placed to promote public goods such as social service provision, economic development and security. This messaging has gone hand-in-hand with 'decampaigns' or with efforts to persuade voters to reject alternative candidates. This multipronged approach is evident in the emphasis commonly placed on a track record of assistance and ability to protect and promote local and national interests, and in the often very personalized attacks on opponents as corrupt, ethnically biased or otherwise morally reprehensible.[44] The increased use of WhatsApp has not fundamentally altered such messaging with important implications for the kinds of information shared and discouraged.

At one level, politicians and their supporters were using 'social media to signal status through interactions with constituents and influential figures' and to 'showcase development activities'.[45] To this end, endorsements by popular or prominent figures were widely shared; characteristics widely regarded as virtuous – such as religious adherence, peace promotion and national pride – were proudly advertised; donations and other forms of local assistance and development support were documented and relayed through pictures and videos; and allegations of wrongdoing were publicly denied.

At another level, the same individuals were using social media to share fake news and negative stories that cast their opponents in a negative light. As one interviewee explained, if 'you are a social media communicator, you have to promote the bad thing to condemn [your opponent's] party. That is the work of the social communicator.'[46] Or, as former president Mahama complained after his defeat in 2016, the NPP 'used a lot of propaganda on social media to tar us with the brush of corruption, incompetence, and telling a lot of tales'.[47]

This common strategy of decampaigning encourages the spread of personalized attacks and fake news, which has become an issue of widespread concern. For example, the Media Foundation for West Africa found that 'more than half of the 98 claims by 2016 electoral campaign participants that it fact-checked were completely false, half-truths, or misleading'.[48] At the same time however, the fact that opponents are constantly looking for ways to decampaign each other helped to curb some of the more dangerous and divisive forms of fake news and propaganda, which could easily prove counter-productive in a context in which both parties need to mobilize support across ethnic, religious, gender and socio-economic lines, and in which there is widespread fear that elections will turn violent and pride in the country's status as the continent's beacon of democracy.[49]

Messaging that was clearly discouraged for these reasons included outright lies that could be relatively easily debunked. As one NDC activist explained:

> When you are campaigning for power you always try to have white propaganda for yourself and black propaganda for your opponent. So, I know anytime you put something on social media, there are people who care to check, [and] when they check and see inaccurate, they will expose you badly![50]

The strength of the opposing party's 'social media army' acted as a deterrent to disseminating outright lies. This also extends to messaging that could be easily presented by opponents as ethnically divisive and destabilizing, and thus as off-putting to a significant number of voters, with party officials fearful of alienating potential swing voters and/or failing to mobilize a maximum turnout of supporters as they sought to secure both a majority of parliamentary seats and the presidential election. In our case study area, this was most evident when it came to chieftaincy disputes, which have long been associated with significant tension and periodic bouts of violence,[51] with discussion of the same widely acknowledged as capable of bringing 'unnecessary tension'.[52] Given a widespread fear of violence, popular commitment to peace, cross-ethnic campaigns,[53] and close races in the region, this common analysis ensured that playing politics with such issues was generally frowned upon and often sanctioned by both local and national figures. As an NPP participant in an inter-party FGD in Nanton noted:

> Some of the platforms are dominated by some particular ethnic [groups] based on the geographic location of the constituency. For example, in northern region here Dagombas are the majority, so if you have the tendency to do chieftaincy politics on the platform, or if you want to do ethnic politics, we may remove you.[54]

He was supported by an NDC communicator who added that this was 'because you may offend the minority'.[55]

Such thinking helped to ensure that such cheap stands as the outright politicization of tribal or chieftaincy politics were often quickly sanctioned. As participants in a FGD in Tamale explained:

> We kicked a lot of people out during our chieftaincy funerals because during that time anyone who tried to politicise our chieftaincy issue we normally gave him warning, we kicked them and to be frank, I can't best remember but we exited a lot of people. We don't tolerate chieftaincy, this tribalism and these religious issues, yes, we don't tolerate them.[56]

This intra-party moderation of social media's potentially more divisive and polarizing tendencies was also evident from the scarcity of explicitly ethnic messaging in recent elections with aspirants and activists 'quick to denounce any aspect of their rival's presidential campaign that suggests a party will favour a particular area – such as [President John] Mahama's comments in 2012 that voters in northern Ghana should support him as a fellow northerner'.[57]

This intra-party moderation is not to suggest that all misleading and divisive propaganda was discouraged. On the contrary, while many feared that disinformation that could easily be debunked might backfire, much information is difficult to prove or disprove with a general perception that politics is a dirty game ensuring that allegations of nepotism and corruption, for example, often appear as highly plausible to a broad range of people. In turn, while explicit promises to co-ethnics and the demonization of ethnic 'others' by candidates and party officials are rare, claims that an opponent is nepotistic, corrupt, incompetent, morally bankrupt, a lapsed Christian or Muslim, or a failed wife or husband constitute a mainstay of everyday political debate.[58]

At the same time, the fact that certain messages might be off-putting to many ordinary voters did not mean that politicians always desisted from using them, but that – when they did – they simply made sure

to distance themselves from such messaging. As one NPP activist
explained:

> Whatever you say on social media, [people] trace back to you. And
> that is why the political figures are not able to do [certain forms of]
> the decampaigning, because it will look like they're involved in politics
> of insults or attacks, instead of portraying the exemplary leadership
> you'll want.

The activist went on to note how – while a politician would know 'that,
if he himself does that, people can also use it to campaign against him
that, "he's intolerant, he's this and he's that, he's always insulting"' –
politicians and activists might use anonymous or fake accounts, or their
supporters, 'to post those things' for the candidate.[59] The strategy here
was simple: an opponent was to be decampaigned without certain types
of more divisive and polarizing messaging being directly traceable to
the candidate or party.

Wider implications

WhatsApp groups have become the favoured platform for intra-
party and candidate organization in Ghana; with impressive reach
and oversight. This has been rendered possible by pre-existing
party structures and informal networks. Indeed, while WhatsApp
organization has become central to political campaigns, it has not
fundamentally altered Ghanaian politics. To be competitive, candidates
still need to be on an NPP or NDC party ticket, and to persuade voters
to turn out and vote for them and against their main opponent. To this
end, candidates still have to 'go to the outdooring',[60] and to display –
a sometimes contradictory mix – of electoral viability, accessibility,
generosity, and civic-mindedness.[61]

   In the Ghanaian context, WhatsApp helps – not only with
logistics and fund-raising – but with strategizing on, and the sharing,
monitoring and controlling, of messaging. Significantly, it does so in

ways that encourage some of the more negative aspects of campaigning in the country – such as fake news and decampaigns – whilst simultaneously helping to check some of the more extreme lies and ethnically or religiously divisive strategies. This is important for intra-group relations and democracy, but once again stems from – rather than produces – the broader political context in which activists and parties are working.

A similar picture is evident in other countries where the increasing use of WhatsApp appears to have reinforced existing party structures, campaign strategies and styles, rather than having transformed them, with very different outcomes depending on the local and national context.[62] The implication of these findings from Ghana and comparative studies is that the (mis)use of social media can never be presumed, but must always be analysed and understood in the particular socio-economic, political and cultural contexts in which it is being adopted and adapted.[63]

Notes

1   Wendy Willems. 2016. 'Beyond free basics: Facebook, data bundles and Zambia's social media internet'. *Africa at LSE*, 1 September. Available at https://blogs.lse.ac.uk/africaatlse/2016/09/01/beyond-free-basics-facebook-data-bundles-and-zambias-social-media-internet/; Toussaint Nothias. 'Access granted: Facebook's free basics in Africa'. *Media Culture & Society* 42, 3 (2020), pp. 329–48.

2   Francis B. Nyamnjoh. 'Globalisation, boundaries and livelihoods: Perspectives on Africa'. *Identity, Culture and Politics* 5, 1&2 (2004), pp. 37–59, p. 53.

3   Wisdom J. Tettey. 'Mobile telephony and democracy in Ghana: Interrogating the changing ecology of citizen engagement and political communication'. *Telecommunications Policy* 41 (2017), pp. 685–94, p. 689.

4   Josephine A. Sanny and Edem Selormey. 'Double-edged sword? Ghanaians see pros, cons of social media, want access but not fake news'. *Afrobarometer Dispatch No. 366* (2020). Available at https://

afrobarometer.org/publications/ad366-ghanaians-see-pros-cons-social-media-want-access-not-fake-news

5   Cornelis Kweku Affre. 2020. 'NPP's savvy use of social media cost me 2016 election – Mahama'. *Joy Online*. 4 December. Available at https://www.myjoyonline.com/npps-savvy-use-of-social-media-cost-me-2016-elections-mahama

6   Interview, NPP communicator, Nanton, 29 June 2019.

7   Ransford Edward Van Gyampo. 'Social media, traditional media and party politics in Ghana'. *Africa Review* 9, 2 (2017), pp. 125–39; Elena Gadjanova, Gabrielle Lynch, Jason Reifler and Ghadafi Saibu. 'Social media, cyber battalions and political mobilization in Ghana' (2019). Available at https://www.elenagadjanova.com/uploads/2/1/3/8/21385412/social_media_cyber_battalions_and_political_mobilisation_in_ghana_report_final.pdf; Nic Cheeseman, Gabrielle Lynch and Justin Willis, *The Moral Economy of Elections in Africa: Democracy, Voting and Virtue* (Cambridge: Cambridge University Press, 2020).

8   Nic Cheeseman, Gabrielle Lynch and Justin Willis. 'Ghana: The ebbing power of incumbency'. *Journal of Democracy* 28, 2 (2017), pp. 92–104; Gadjanova et al. 'Social media, cyber battalions and political mobilization in Ghana'; Van Gyampo, 'Social media, traditional media and party politics in Ghana'; Nic Cheeseman, Jonathan Fisher, Idayat Hassan and Jamie Hitchen. 'Social media disruption: Nigeria's WhatsApp politics'. *Journal of Democracy* 31, 3 (2020), pp. 145–59; Akwasi Bosompem Boateng, Donal Patrick McCracken and Musara Lubombo. 'Intra-party election campaigns in Ghana: An analysis of Facebook use'. in Martin N. Ndlela and Winston Mano (eds), *Social Media and Elections in Africa: Theoretical Perspectives and Election Campaigns* (Cham: Palgrave Macmillan, 2020), pp. 215–32.

9   Jonathan Corpus Ong and Jason Vincent A. Cabañes, *Architects of Networked Disinformation: Behind the Scenes of Troll Accounts and Fake News Production in the Philippines* (Leeds: University of Leeds, Newton Tech4Dev Network, 2018). Available at https://newtontechfordev.com/wp-content/uploads/2018/02/ARCHITECTS-OF-NETWORKED-DISINFORMATION-FULL-REPORT.pdf

10 In 2016 and 2020, the NDC secured Tamale Central, North and South, and the NPP Nanton.

11 In 2016 the presidential vote was divided thus: Tamale Central 62 per cent NDC and 37 per cent NPP; Tamale North 74 per cent NDC and 25 per cent NPP; Tamale South 72 per cent NDC and 26 per cent NPP; and Nanton 50 per cent NDC and 49 per cent NPP. In 2020 the presidential vote was divided thus: Tamale Central 61 per cent NDC and 37 per cent NPP; Tamale North 69 per cent NDC and 30 per cent NPP; Tamale South 68 per cent NDC and 30 per cent; and Nanton 46 per cent NDC and 53 per cent NPP.

12 For example, see Paul Nugent. 'Living in the past: Rural, urban and ethnic themes in the 1992 and 1996 elections in Ghana'. *Journal of Modern African Studies* 37, 2 (1999), pp. 287–319; Joseph R. A. Ayee. 'Manifestos and elections in Ghana's Fourth Republic'. *South African Journal of International Affairs* 15, 2 (2011), pp. 185–214; Sebastian Elischer. 'Measuring and comparing party ideology in nonindustrialized societies: Taking party manifesto research to Africa'. *Democratization* 19, 4 (2012), pp. 642–67; Noah L. Nathan, *Electoral Politics and Africa's Urban Transition: Class and Ethnicity in Ghana* (Cambridge: Cambridge University Press, 2019).

13 European Union Election Observation Mission Ghana. *Presidential and Parliamentary Elections, December 7 2020: Preliminary Statement* (9 December 2020), p. 7. Available at https://eeas.europa.eu/sites/default/files/eueom_ghana_preliminary_statement_.pdf

14 Nugent. 'Living in the past'; Lindsay Whitfield. 'Change for a better Ghana: Party competition, institutionalization and alternation in Ghana's 2008 elections'. *African Affairs* 108, 433 (2009), pp. 621–41; Ayee. 'Manifestos and elections in Ghana's Fourth Republic'; Cyril K. Daddieh and George M. Bob-Milliar. 'In search of "honorable" membership: Parliamentary primaries and candidate selection in Ghana'. *Journal of Asian and African Studies* 47, 2 (2012), pp. 204–20.

15 The NDC has gone from securing all of the parliamentary seats in Northern Ghana in 1992, to sharing the seats with the NPP in the 2016 and 2020 elections (9 seats each).

16 George Bob-Milliar. 'Place and party organizations: Party activism inside party-branded sheds at the grassroots in northern Ghana'. *Territory, Politics, Governance* 7, 4 (2019), pp. 474–93.

17 Kevin S. Fridy and Victor Brobbey. 'The match and vote for me: The politicisation of Ghana's Accra Hearts of Oak and Kumasi Asante

Kotoko football clubs'. *Journal of Modern African Studies* 47, 1 (2009), pp. 19–39; George Bob-Milliar. 'Political party activism in Ghana: Factors influencing the decision of the politically active to join a political party'. *Democratization* 19, 4 (2012), pp. 668–89.

18 Interview, NPP youth group member, Tamale North constituency, 15 June 2019.

19 Gadjanova et al. 'Social media, cyber battalions and political mobilization in Ghana', p. 10.

20 Interview, NDC executive member, Nanton, 1 July 2019.

21 Interview, Convention People's Party youth organizer, Accra, 15 July 2019.

22 Interview, NDC executive, Accra, 22 March 2019.

23 Interview, NDC MP, Accra, 12 July 2019.

24 Interview, radio presenter, Tamale, 19 July 2019.

25 Wisdom J. Tettey. 'Talk radio and politics in Ghana: Exploring civic and (un)civil discourse in the public sphere'. in L. Gunner, D. Moyo and D. Ligaga (eds), *Radio in Africa: Cultures, Publics and Communities* (Johannesburg: Wits University Press, 2011), pp. 19–35.

26 Interview, NDC leader, Accra, 20 March 2019.

27 Cheeseman et al. *The Moral Economy of Elections in Africa.*

28 Cf. Stephen Ellis. 'Tuning in to pavement radio'. *African Affairs* 88, 352 (1989), pp. 321–30, p. 321; see Elena Gadjanova, Gabrielle Lynch and Ghadafi Saibu. 'Pavement radio in the social media age: How misinformation crosses digital divides in Northern Ghana'. Working Paper (2021).

29 Gadjanova et al. 'Social media, cyber battalions and political mobilization in Ghana'. p. 13.

30 Boateng et al. 'Intra-party election campaigns in Ghana', p. 224.

31 Jennifer Stromer-Galley. *Presidential Campaigning in the Internet Age* (Oxford: Oxford University Press, 2019), pp. 2 and 3 (emphasis in the original).

32 Interview, NPP communicator, Tamale, 18 July 2019.

33 FGD, NPP member, Tamale, 24 June 2019.

34 FGD, Nanton, 29 June 2019.

35 FGD, NPP communicator, Nanton, 29 June 2019.

36 Interview, NPP youth, Tamale, 18 June 2019.

37 Interview, NPP communicator, Nanton, 29 June 2019.

38 FGD, NDC organizer, Nanton, 29 June 2019.
39 Interview, NDC communicator, Accra, 14 March 2019.
40 Interview, NPP leader, Accra, 16 July 2019.
41 FGD NPP communicator, Nanton, 29 June 2019.
42 FGD, NPP communicator, Tamale, 24 June 2019.
43 Interview, NPP communicator, Nanton, 29 June 2019.
44 Paul Nugent. 'Winners, losers and also rans: Money, moral authority and voting patterns in the Ghana 2000 elections'. *African Affairs* 100, 400 (2001), pp. 405–28; Elena Gadjanova. 'Electoral clientelism as status affirmation in Africa: Evidence from Ghana'. *Journal of Modern African Studies* 55, 4 (2017), pp. 593–621; Cheeseman et al. *The Moral Economy of Elections in Africa*.
45 Gadjanova et al. 'Social media, cyber battalions and political mobilization in Ghana'. p. 3.
46 Interview, NDC youth group member, Tamale, 14 June 2019.
47 Affre. 'NPP's savvy use of social media cost me 2016 election – Mahama'.
48 Sanny and Selormey. 'Double-edged sword?'. p. 1.
49 Gabrielle Lynch, Nic Cheeseman and Justin Willis. 'From peace campaigns to peaceocracy: Elections, order and authority in Africa'. *African Affairs* 118, 473 (2019), pp. 603–27.
50 Interview, NPP party activist, Nanton, 23 July 2019.
51 Jesse Salah Ovadia. 'Stepping back from the brink: A review of the 2008 Ghanaian election from the capital of the northern region'. *Canadian Journal of African Studies* 45, 2 (2011), pp. 310–40.
52 Interview, NPP party activist, Nanton, 23 July 2019.
53 See Elena Gadjanova. 'Status-quo or grievance coalitions: The logic of cross-ethnic campaign appeals in Africa's highly diverse states'. *Comparative Political Studies* 54, 3 (2020), pp. 652–85.
54 FGD, NPP official, Nanton, 29 June 2019.
55 FGD, NDC organizer, Nanton, 29 June 2019.
56 FGD Youth Group, youth group member, Tamale, 24 June 2019.
57 Cheeseman et al. *The Moral Economy of Elections in Africa*, p. 242.
58 Ibid.
59 Interview, journalist, Tamale, 19 July 2019.
60 Cited in Gadjanova et al. 'Social media, cyber battalions and political mobilization in Ghana'. p. 13.

61 Cheeseman et al. *The Moral Economy of Elections in Africa*.

62 Cheeseman et al. 'Social media disruption'.; Eloïse Betrand, Grace
    Natabaalo and Jamie Hitchen. *Connecting with Constituents?
    Parliamentary Aspirants' Use of WhatsApp in Uganda's 2021 'Scientific'
    Election*. Westminster Foundation for Democracy (May 2021). Available
    at https://www.wfd.org/wp-content/uploads/2021/06/Parliamentary-
    aspirants-use-of-WhatsApp-in-Ugandas-2021-elections.pdf.

63 For example, see Maggie Dwyer and Thomas Molony (eds). *Social Media
    and Politics in Africa: Democracy, Censorship and Security* (London: Zed
    Books, 2019); Sharath Srinivasan, R. Stephanie Diepeveen and George
    Karekwaivanane. 'Rethinking publics in Africa in a digital age'. *Journal of
    Eastern African Studies* 13, 1 (2019), pp. 2–17; Cheeseman et al. 'Social
    media disruption'.

2

WhatsApp, youth and politics in the Gambia: An analysis of 'Democratic Gambia'

Sait Matty Jaw

Globally, the space provided by the internet for networking and debate is promoting the active political participation of young people. It has given rise to new movements, active both online and offline – that are challenging political establishments such as #BringBackOurGirls in Nigeria. The advent and rise of social media platforms such as Twitter, and its use in the Arab Spring, have intensified the debate on what effect these tools can have in transforming authoritarian regimes into democratic ones.[1] Questions about how social media might strengthen societal challenges to authoritarian rule and how these challenges to authoritarian rule translate into actual political changes on the ground are shaping debates about the role that internet can play in democratic transition in non-democratic regimes.

In the Gambia, the internet, social media platforms and private messenger applications supported activists in the diaspora and at home to engage in a protracted struggle against the regime of Yahya Jammeh. From the start in 1994, initially through various platforms including listservs, online radios and papers, and then increasingly through Facebook and WhatsApp, the diaspora remained connected and engaged with homeland politics and involved in raising funds to support opposition parties and movements. The limited space, for opposition or dissent coupled with Jammeh's gradual consolidation of

Sait Matty Jaw is lecturer in the department of political science, University of The Gambia, Brikama.

power, shifted political activism online where it was predominantly led by vocal members of the diaspora. But as the digital space developed, Gambian online activism began to shift to accommodate the new tools, and even utilized them to advance their struggle to restore democracy by improving connections with local activists.

The Gambia has an influential diaspora of as many as 200,000 – around 10 per cent of its total population – that contributed 22 per cent of GDP in 2016.[2] The mobilization efforts by politically active diaspora led to the establishment of various movements loosely known as the 'struggle' which emerged with the goal of restoring democracy in the Gambia.[3] Although it had been organizing multiparty elections since independence,[4] the country had never registered an electoral turnover until 2016 when current president, Adama Barrow, defeated Jammeh.

Although the online movement was rooted in the diaspora and had effectively internationalized Gambian politics through protest and lobbying host governments as well as international organizations, its ability to have a transformative impact within the Gambia had been limited by the oppressive nature of the Jammeh regime. In 2001, Jammeh changed the electoral law from an absolute majority to a simple majority. A move that meant unless Gambia's political opposition could unite, it would struggle to defeat him. However, the dynamics began to change when local activists and diaspora activists collaborated in the run-up to the 2016 election, largely through WhatsApp. WhatsApp, unlike Facebook and other open platforms, provided more security for grassroots activists in the country. I was part of and central to many of these organizations and movements. I was a key member of #NewGambiaMovement and was one of the first people added to #DemocraticGambia WhatsApp group. I was also was one of the first to benefit from a viral social media campaign – #FreeSaitMattyJaw – that demanded my release from detention in 2014.

This chapter explores the emergence, evolution and nature of WhatsApp groups as a tool for youth activism in the Gambia. Using key informant interviews, desk research and my own observations and experiences,[5] it assesses how a locally grown movement on WhatsApp emerged at the height of Jammeh's autocratic rule. Focusing on the engagement and mobilization efforts it explores how WhatsApp allowed for diaspora activists and on the ground activist to discuss, engage and organize, and how such groups influenced local politics in the run-up to, and in the aftermath of, the transformative 2016 election.

Mobilizing on WhatsApp

Young Gambian activists' decision to shift their attention to the political landscape followed continental consultation on youth participation and leadership as well as the emergence of the 'Not Too Young to Run' movement in Nigeria. A National Youth Parliament–led conversation on youth political participation and leadership held at the American Corner[6] in October 2015 was the initial spark. The conversation, which was carried out in three stages, was part of continental consultation by the African Governance Architecture secretariat under the department of political affairs at the African Union.[7]

The first stage of these discussions saw the creation of a WhatsApp group comprising activists from various youth groups across the country to discuss the best approach to increase youth political participation and leadership. In addition, a face-to-face dialogue on the topic was organized that brought together youth activists and youth from across political parties to unpack key issues. Following these discussions, it was agreed that a WhatsApp group must exist as a platform to continue the debate and that membership was to be expanded to include others, beyond participants that attended the forum at the American Corner.[8]

The WhatsApp group was initially named the Progressive Youth Network. All the youth activists interviewed for this chapter acknowledged that this was the first group that was created aimed at discussing politics in the Gambia and at getting youth more involved in politics. The Network was envisaged as a non-partisan platform that was to enable and support engagement with political parties and other stakeholders to implement the recommendations and resolutions from the youth workshop. At the initial stages the group was primarily focused on discussing ways and strategies to increase youth participation and how to go about establishing national structures to pursue the goal of improved access to leadership.

But plans to register as a formal youth network, to legitimize the movement but also to protect themselves against the regime, failed. Despite a constitution and other by-laws and strategies being developed to engage political actors, the Network was never registered due to government screening. According to the Network's Chairperson, Absa Samba:

> We even drafted the constitution that we were going to use to register the group but then again, the group did not get registered because the government started asking a lot of questions about who we are.[9]

The activists tried to be very strategic in their engagement with the regime. Unlike the diaspora that was openly confrontational, they were careful with the language they used so as not to look confrontational and draw attention. For instance, in their constitution which was to be submitted to the Attorney General Chambers for registration the group state that their mission was 'to create a vibrant society through the participation and engagement of youth in national development by complimenting the efforts of government and relevant stakeholders'.[10] This reflected the language of the regime, which deemed anything not in support of national development as a threat that could be met with arrest and torture.[11] But the group did not escape the attentions of the government for long once it started to champion opposition political coalitions in August 2016.

> We were very strategic with the language we use just so we didn't look confrontational and avoided been watched and stuff. We think that changed when we were doing the campaign ... for example, Pierre Minteh who was then at the embassy in DC came after me and was like do not bite the hand that feed you ... all I did was merely ask the opposition parties to form a coalition to get rid of Jammeh.[12]

In addition to these more strategic activities, events, specifically the response to the murder of United Democratic Party (UDP) National Youth Mobiliser Solo Sandeng in April 2016 at the hands of state security forces, saw WhatsApp mobilization come to the fore. The death of Sandeng highlighted the reason why many young people refused to participate in politics; the political terrain was a site of violent state repression. Whilst it energized youth activists they could not agree as to the best way forward and the heated debate on WhatsApp and elsewhere that ensued led to its gradual demise. On the one hand were people calling for a 'Gambian Spring', and on the other side were people that were still focused on making incremental election gains.

On 16 April 2016 Ibraheem Ceesay, a member of the Network and Chairman of the National Youth Council, posted a picture on his Facebook wall with #JammehMustGo visibly written on his palm. In the same post, he called on Gambians, particularly the youth, to take to the streets in peaceful protest on Monday, 18 April 2016.

> My fellow Gambians, especially the youth, as your Chairman and Youth Leader, lets get to the streets on Monday 18 April 2016, for a PEACEFUL protest to demand #Justice for #SoloSandeng and to ALL brave Gambians arrested #JammehMustGo #Exodus #LetsDoItForTheGambia #Shalom.[13]

Ceesay's post marked the beginning of local activists' publicly demanding for regime change. To pursue his ideas for protest, Ceesay created a WhatsApp group (#NewGambiaMovement) which included leading activists in the Gambia and across the diaspora, including the current Minister of Youth and Sports, Bakary Badjie. The movement's goal was simple: #JammehMustGo. Through the WhatsApp group, activists strategized and shared live information about the protests. The date, time and location of the protest were communicated on the platform and then spread through a multitude of WhatsApp groups that grew in number with the protests. When the protesters were on the streets, WhatsApp was used to communicate and locate other protesters or even to inform group members about the whereabouts of the security forces. For instance, Lamin K. Saidy, who was one of the leaders of the group on the ground, and is now deputy youth mobilizer for President Barrow's National People's Party, was constantly updating the group on what was happening and sharing pictures of the measures that were being taken by the Police Intervention Unit.

However, the death of Sandeng, and the protests that followed, not only highlighted the violent nature of the Jammeh regime, but also exposed the weak and disorganized nature of Gambian civil society and political activists. Even though they were united in their goals, the movement was not cohesive. According to prominent musician Killa Ace, who himself was in exile in Senegal for releasing songs critical of Jammeh,

> unfortunately, there isn't a youth movement that's structured to social awareness. If that were available, it would be like the movement in Burkina Faso, where people spoke up as one force. But if you speak up individually, it won't work.[14]

In response to President Blaise Compaoré's attempt to amend the constitution to extend his twenty-seven-year rule in Burkina Faso, civil society mobilized tens of thousands of citizens to demand his resignation in 2014. For many like Killa Ace, the popular movement that eventually toppled the Compaoré regime was the ideal to be emulated in the Gambia as they had lost hope in the ability of elections to deliver change. However, Gambian activists and movements on the ground in country did not have this sort of grassroots base on which they could call. It remained loose and predominantly virtual. But that began to shift ahead of the 2016 election.

Supporting a collective political voice

The WhatsApp forum that later became known as 'Democratic Gambia' was created to pursue and support electoral objectives agreed by youth activists at a series of offline meetings. Although the group was created first to advance political discussions, it subsequently became a mobilization tool for a united opposition coalition. Young activists were key supporters and advocates for the opposition coalition. In August 2016, after a couple of months of behind the scenes lobbying, they went public with this support. Foroyaa journalist Kebba Jeffang, a member of the WhatsApp group, interviewed several other members to gain their views on the coalition. The strategy was adopted to ensure that no one took responsibility and for it to look like random people making random contributions when it has all been planned on the WhatsApp forum. According to the article, which was published on 10 August, a handful of young people across the country called on all opposition parties to unite ahead of the election to remove Jammeh.[15]

> Kemo Bojang, another young man, told Foroyaa that unity among the opposition parties is now or never, as clock is ticking with less than 4 months before the Presidential election on the 1 December, this year. He said the country needs a change of government after over 22 years of APRC [Alliance for Patriotic Reorientation and Construction] government and the only way to do this is through a coalition where all the opposition parties will come together and contest against the incumbent.[16]

> We are calling all the opposition parties to come together and produce a coalition for change. They need to combine their forces in order to effect necessary and desired change in the Gambia. I feel it is better for us to have a grand coalition rather than each of the opposition parties contesting to remove the incumbent from power.[17]

Initially youth backing was offered to Dr Isatou Touray, an individual with a strong activist background, who promised to serve just one five-year term if elected, as a 'transitional president'. But after she withdrew from the opposition-led discussions about who should front the coalition, members of the group threw their support behind Adama Barrow, the individual selected to head up the coalition. The group name changed from 'Support Dr Touray' to 'Forward with Gambia' and in addition to changing the name of the group, members decided to petition her, in the end successfully, to join the united front to avoid a scenario where opposition votes were divided. The petition was discussed and shared in the WhatsApp group and was captured and reported by journalists in the group.[18]

> We the young people of the Gambia that supported her throughout, call on Dr. Touray to suspend her nomination and join the opposition coalition for the future of Gambia. This is not the time to bring division. We call for unity. We respect you and understand how much you are willing to do for Gambia. What we as young people want right now is change and a hopeful future were we can thrive and be the best we can be. The only way for us now is the opposition coalition. We appeal to you to hear us out and respect our voice and demand.[19]

WhatsApp became instrumental for the opposition political campaign and for the activists that were supporting Barrow's candidacy. As an alternative to the state-dominated Gambia Radio and Television Service, WhatsApp became the voice of the opposition and those interested in regime change. Many WhatsApp groups were created to improve communication and the flow of information. This made it possible for the diaspora and home-based activists to exchange ideas and share campaign materials. Mola Kambi, a member of the group, recalled that:

> Through this medium, campaign materials such as images, news articles, audio messages were shared. Because there were so many WhatsApp groups, Gambians everywhere easily had access to the materials. Even though there were restrictions at some points on the internet, we did [not] waiver. We downloaded VPNs. We kept fighting.[20]

The Gambian diaspora generated funds for the opposition allowing them to better navigate the huge finances involved in electioneering, particularly when Jammeh increased the fees to contest in presidential election to half a million Dalasi (almost US$10,000). In total the diaspora raised almost US$150,000, which was used to fund opposition campaigning. Not enough to compete with Jammeh, but a significant amount that would have been hard to raise in-country alone.

Unlike GoFundme and Facebook Live that were used to raise funds for opposition efforts, WhatsApp was largely used to try to demystify

Jammeh through sharing leaked and concocted information, even if some of the viral stories that circulated – like that of babies being sacrificed – were false.[21] Caricatures of Jammeh and photoshopped images were shared regularly. Journalist Alhagie Abdoulie Ceesay of Taranga Radio was even arrested for sharing a picture of Jammeh with a gun pointed at his head on WhatsApp.[22] A lot of the claims started on diaspora media houses before being widely shared through an increasing number of WhatsApp forums.

The information shared on the WhatsApp forums helped mobilize youth to turnout on the campaign trail as well as to register and then go and vote. WhatsApp was instrumental as it helped facilitate direct engagement between diaspora activists and their family, neighbours, friends and community members in the Gambia. Activists produced tailor-made audio messages that were shared through WhatsApp with their networks back home; messages that encouraged them to vote for the coalition candidate Adama Barrow. Then living in Norway, I also participated in such processes using WhatsApp to convince my extended family members to vote for the coalition candidate. WhatsApp became very important for the diaspora activists due to the way it improved communications at a low cost. It enabled diaspora activists to support constituency and local level voter mobilization.

For example, in Central River Division, the largest of the five administrative divisions in the Gambia, there were separate WhatsApp groups for each constituency with teams of volunteers on motorbikes and cars shuttling messages to key voters and voting blocks and extracting firm commitments of support for the coalition candidate. Illustrating how WhatsApp enabled online mobilization that could have offline impacts as many of the voters reached by the volunteers had no access to the internet or even mobile phones. It was very efficient in the micro-targeting of electors to the extent that activists believed they could count the votes we were likely to get even before the first ballot was cast.

The day before the election, the Jammeh regime shut down the internet and international calls,[23] making it practically impossible for the diaspora and home-based activists to communicate. Even the WhatsApp group was quiet, becoming more active only a couple of days later when connection was partially restored. But as Gambians came back online, many were surprised to learn that not only had President Jammeh lost the election, but he also appeared willing to concede defeat. However Jammeh subsequently changed his mind and publicly rejected the election results, claiming that malpractice had led to his defeat.[24] In the six weeks that followed, social media was again instrumental in shaping the Gambia's political trajectory.

#GambiaHasDecided became a rallying call for citizen activists and members of 'Forward with Gambia' were instrumental in making the call for Jammeh to leave go viral through their WhatsApp platform. The organizing was not just limited to online. Some of the members volunteered and started distributing #GambiaHasDecided T-shirts to protestors. The greater visibility of members was not without its perils though as some were targeted by the regime as it tried to cling to power and were forced to flee to Senegal. WhatsApp groups were again a key medium through which activists could keep in contact, keep each other informed and sustain the momentum needed to ensure Jammeh was forced to accept the election outcome. In January, facing domestic pressure and after a series of negotiations with Economic Community of West African States representatives Jammeh left for exile in Equatorial Guinea.

Following the departure of Jammeh, the WhatsApp group evolved again to Democratic Gambia with the primary aim of promoting and deepening democracy in the Gambia. However, these ideals have not been realized. Due to the growing partisanship of Gambian politics, the group has turned into a platform where different individuals with partisan interest debate partisan politics. A participant noted that the group just like other diaspora groups established to bring about regime change – for which they could agree on a united goal – does not contribute much to national politics as its membership has become obsessed with political partisanship. He noted that 'one of the biggest challenges is that members are too aligned to their party politics'.[25] The political affiliation of members was not a factor when the group was created in 2016 but under the more liberal political environment that has emerged, members have either found new, or revealed existing, political party allegiances.

Gambia's WhatsApp politics

Political activism associated with the internet has contributed significantly to the political trajectory of the Gambia in the last decade. It has emerged as a new public sphere, a home of anti-regime protest and a place where home-based and diaspora-based activists can connect. Due to state control of public space, social media and private messenger applications became the only space for citizens to access and exchange ideas and information.[26] WhatsApp was crucial to this networked public as seen with the rise of many WhatsApp groups that were created to coordinate opposition political party activities efforts and share information about their electoral commitments at all levels.

> These WhatsApp groups became influential platforms where targeted voice messages were sent and shared across platforms. With voice messages, the illiteracy challenge was overcome, as one would see old men and women in the villages listening to these messages. This helped to energise electorates and encourage them to vote. The use of the internet through social media and online media outlets became the single most powerful tool that mobilised and organised the people at all levels to stand up to Jammeh.[27]

Undoubtedly, WhatsApp with its facilities was critical in efforts aimed at ending two decades of autocratic rule by Jammeh. It enabled activities to circumvent the public space, whether they could never have taken place, without losing their direct and intimate engagement. But as the Gambia grapples with its new-found freedom, WhatsApp has become very instrumental in the spread of fake news, often driven by ethnic or political agendas.

A recent study showed how WhatsApp, and social media platforms like Facebook, are continuing to shape Gambian politics directly and indirectly post Jammeh.[28] In showing how hashtag activism in the Gambia translates into offline movements such as #OccupyWestfield,[29] it observed that WhatsApp is the leading online platform to share information in the Gambia and that most forums on WhatsApp 'replicate offline organisations online; built around faith networks, family structures, political allegiances or community or education associations'.[30] Noting that through the audio facility provided by WhatsApp, local languages such as Wolof and Mandinka have become effective and persistent in the information sharing eco-system. This has been recognized by political actors too. All political parties have created networks of WhatsApp groups, stretching down to the ward level, as mediums for communication, mobilization and even fund-raising, and these are set to play an important role in the future political direction of the country.

Notes

1　Zeynep Tufekci. *Twitter and Tear Gas: The Power and Fragility of Networked Protest* (New Haven: Yale University Press, 2018).

2　Ebrima Sawaneh. 2017. 'Gambia relies on migrant's remittances for 22% of GDP-IFAD reports'. Business in Gambia. 23 June.

3　Sait Matty Jaw. 2017. 'Restoring democracy in the Gambia: An analysis of diaspora engagement in Gambian politics'. Unpublished Master's Thesis. University of Bergen, Norway.

4　The People Progressive Party and Sir Dawada Kairaba Jawara won all election in Gambia since independence. Following the military transition Jammeh also won all the election except 2016 when he was defeated by Barrow.

5　I have been a key member of activist groups in the Gambia for over a decade.

6　The American Corner is a public library under the US Embassy Public Affairs Division. I was part of the first interns of the corner given the task of promoting the space to the public. The corner soon became a free space for activists to meet, discuss as well as organize events. It is still functioning and continues to be a go to place for young activists.

7   I led the first AGA consultation while in exile. On this occasion I supported the process from afar.

8   Interview with Samba Bah, 10 January 2021.

9   Interview with Absa Samba, 5 January 2021.

10 Draft Constitution of Progressive Youth Network.

11 I was arrested in November 2014 in connection with a Gallop Poll study. The question that got me arrested was one asking whether people approve or disapprove Jammeh. I knew the question was problematic given the context, but I still advised the group to go ahead given that at that time I was interested in understanding the approval ratings of Jammeh. We were arrested and detained for more than the 72 hours stipulated by the constitution. I was released but then re-arrested and charged. After a six-month trial, I was acquitted and discharged by the magistrate court. After this ruling I escaped to Senegal pending my visa application to relocate to Norway for studies under the Student's at Risk programme. I returned to Gambia in 2017. While away I was still connected to the activists at home who had carried out a vibrant social media campaign for my release. Moving to the diaspora also enabled me to connect and understand both worlds and my positionality enabled me to explore the role of the diaspora in political mobilisation.

12 Interview with Absa Samba, 5 January 2021.

13 Ibraheem Ceesay. Facebook Post. 16 April 2016.

14 Louise Hunt. 2016. 'Young Gambians are ready to vote out dictatorial Yahya Jammeh regime'. *The Guardian*. 30 November. Available at https://www.theguardian.com/global-development/2016/nov/30/young-gambians-ready-to-vote-out-dictatorial-yahya-jammeh-regime

15 Kebba Jeffang. 2016. Young people task Opposition Leaders to Unite. *Foroyaa*. 10 August.

16 Jeffang, 'Young people task opposition'.

17 Ibid.

18 Mustapha K. Darboe. 2016. 'Dr. Touray petitioned by supporters to join coalition'. *The Torch*. 2 November.

19 Quoted from the petition 'Dr. Isatou Touray must suspend her campaign: Join coalition now'. *Change.Org*. Available at https://www.change.org/p/

dr-isatou-touray-dr-isatou-touray-must-suspend-her-camapaign-join-
the-coalition-now

20	Interview with Mola Kambia, 15 January 2021.

21	Musa Saidykhan. 2016. 'Why Jammeh is kidnapping children'. *Kairo
News*. 7 November.

22	Community to Protect Journalists. 2016. 'Gambian Journalist Sentenced
to two years in prison'. 23 November.

23	Abdi Latif Dahir. 2016. 'Gambia's government has shut down the internet
on the eve of election'. *Quartz Africa*. 1 December.

24	Umaru Fofana. 2016. 'Jammeh's U-turn over Gambia elections causes
row'. *BBC News*. 13 December.

25	Interview with Durosimi Taylor, 1 February 2021.

26	Sait Matty Jaw. 2017. Victory for ACDEG: The Gambia's Post Election
Crisis and Lesson for Africa in Africa's Demographic Dividends and
Deficits. African Governance Newsletter. AGA. January–June.

27	Jaw. 'Victory for ACDEG'.

28	Idayat Hassan and Jamie Hitchen. 2020. 'Forums of debate? WhatsApp
and the Gambia's Political Transition'. CDD West Africa. September.

29	#OccupyWestfield was the first protest to take place under the new
government in November 2017 against water and electricity shortages in
urban areas. Organized by young people, it gained momentum online and
relied heavily on Facebook for mobilization.

30	Hassan and Hitchen. 'Forums of debate'.

3

WhatsApp political campaigns in Nigeria

Nwachukwu Egbunike

The influence of digital media on Nigeria's democratic landscape has garnered considerable scholarship in recent years.[1] Digital media in Nigeria politics was evident as far back as the 2011 general elections, where an interconnected network of online citizens broadened their political participation and voter behaviour.[2] The proliferation of digital spaces increased the political discourse and made it more participatory.[3] The 2015 election saw an attempt to fully interrogate the place and true influence of digital media in elections in Nigeria. But despite this growing influence, social media did not provide as much support for Nigeria's democratic transformation during the 2015 elections as Nigeria's well-rooted organized labour movement did.[4] It was claimed that the leadership of the Nigerian Labour Congress, the umbrella of all trade unions in the country, had 'the capacity to sway their support in any direction' of any of the 2015 presidential candidates.[5]

In the 2019 general election, social media again grew in prominence, acting as an expressive and influential resource for youth mobilization and participation.[6] Bello et al.[7] correctly predicted the outcome of the 2019 elections in twenty-four states out of the thirty-six states plus Abuja, the capital city, through sentiment analysis of major Twitter handles of political parties and their candidates. This suggests that online and offline worlds are becoming more connected than ever before. But social media's influence has not always been positive. Digital media propelled, disseminated and legitimatized misinformation and

Nwachukwu Egbunike is an adjunct lecturer at the School of Media and Communication, Pan Atlantic University, Lagos.

disinformation during the 2019 elections.[8] Twitter, for example, was a landmine of ethnocentric disinformation and propaganda prior to, during and after the 2019 vote.[9]

But the influence of digital media is not limited to elections alone. It has also been impactful during charged periods of political protest in Nigeria and beyond.[10] Digital media provided the space for dissent and resistance by Nigerian youths against the increase in the cost of petrol, which eventually spiralled into the 2012 #OccupyNigeria protests.[11] However in this instance, print media provided a more authentic narrative of the protesters' message than social media. Social media users, to validate the energy of the protests, amplified deviant behaviour of protesters burning tires and engaging in violence. Unfortunately, this led to an attrition of the message which the mass action wished to portray.[12] Eight years after the #OccupyNigeria protests, young Nigerians were once again on the streets protesting police brutality. The social media–mediated national protests trended on Twitter with the hashtag #EndSARS, and soon morphed into offline demonstrations. #EndSARS protests saw an overlap of online and offline efforts through the raising of funds, and provision of legal help and logistics online.[13]

The growing influence of digital media on elections and activism in Nigeria is significant. However, most of scholarship in this area to date has been Twitter-centric.[14] This can be explained by the fact that whilst storytelling on Twitter is essentially public,[15] that of WhatsApp, like all private messenger applications, are usually private and therefore harder to access.[16] But WhatsApp is an increasingly important online tool for political mobilization in the country. As Cheeseman et al.[17] demonstrated, it was utilized in 2019 for the spread of politicized mis/disinformation through semi-structured organizations affiliated with, but formally separate from, the two leading presidential candidates. This study will seek to further interrogate the use of WhatsApp in political campaigning in Nigeria to better understand how the application is used to share political messaging, how falsehoods and propaganda circulate, and to appreciate how valuable the tool is seen to be by party activists and campaign strategists.

A User and Gratification (U&G) theoretical framework is applied to conduct the analysis. U&G theory is audience-based, looking at the people involved in a communicative process. It is interested in what people do with the media and not what the media does to them. Studies that engage this theorical framework were historically limited to the study of traditional media.[18] However, digital media scholarship has resuscitated the interest in U&G theory: from interpersonal communication on digital platforms to online marketing, or the need of an understanding of why audiences use the digital media.[19]

Five participants[20] who were interviewed for this study were selected through a purposive non-random or judgemental sampling of former election campaign or media managers of different political candidates, across the Nigerian political spectrum. The sample size for this study is sufficient based on these three reasons. The first is that general elections in Nigeria are held every four years and WhatsApp became prominent in Nigeria's political campaigns only during the 2015 vote. Since then, Nigeria has had only one general election, in 2019. This is in addition to several off-cycle governorship elections. This means that there is already a limited sample size of qualified participants who were involved in these elections. The second reason is that since these participants form a homogenous group, as former political campaign officials, a smaller sample size is required.[21] Third, this study is focused on investigating the contextual meaning that participants ascribed to their lived experience of using WhatsApp for political campaigns in Nigeria.[22]

Employing WhatsApp for political messaging

All the participants admitted that WhatsApp helped them to mobilize and spread the political messages of their candidates during election campaigns. The application aided their work in delivering deliberate political campaigns, through direct, targeted and personalized messaging aimed at voters. It also helped in reaching out to delegates to coordinate activities. 'It's easy to take it for granted now because so many things are now within our reach,' asserted one political campaign adviser.[23] But it was not so in 2014 at the early stages of the digital democratization of the media ecology in Nigeria. WhatsApp became a game changer for election campaigns in Nigeria only during the 2015 presidential election. According to political strategist Ose Anenih:

> Up until that point we were all use[d] to the old style of politicking, it would be rallies, radio jingles and TV adverts. But in the run to the 2015 election, Twitter was already in Nigeria, Facebook was in Nigeria, WhatsApp was in Nigeria.[24]

WhatsApp campaigns became more prevalent and strategic in the 2016 and 2017 governorship elections in Edo and Anambra states respectively:

> After the 2015 election which we lost, we sort of took lessons. The next year we had the Edo state election, I deliberately set out to use WhatsApp to influence and help my candidate's campaign.[25]

> Let's say, we have X number of voters in a state or local government. But the bulk of the voting population are civil servants who are compelled to be registered … These are critical insight to now prepare and draft messages to a specific demography. So, there are different approaches, but WhatsApp was really useful, because it was an easy way to reach out and again.[26]

But it was not until 2019 that targeted messaging became a feature of WhatsApp campaigning:

> What we did in 2019, initially it met some resistance but as we drew closer to the election people directly got news from us on how to vote, people got direct news from us on why they should vote for our candidate. People were able to communicate with us. And there were able to do this in the comfort of their house across different parts of the country in their own language.[27]

> In 2019, both parties invested hundreds of millions of Naira in technology in setting up social media and contact rooms. So, for the first time they digitalised the voters register. When you talk about

targeted messaging, you have a database of everyone that will take part in the election. And for the first time you were able to send targeted WhatsApp messages to these people based on where they are. The virtual database is not just grouped based on age, gender but also around occupation, location. You are able to send a certain type of message to the southeast, send a different message to northeast, or send a different message to northwest. I hadn't seen any campaign use that type of messaging up until 2019 when both sides did.[28]

That WhatsApp was used to send targeted and personalized messages which used demographic information and contact details like mobile phone numbers and place of residence which are all captured in the voters' register is notable. How their campaign office or political party was able to access such detailed information about voters in the first place was not disclosed by participants, but there are unsubstantiated rumours that staff at telecoms firms sell subscriber details, with regulation covering data protection and data privacy in Nigeria weak. The consequence of this more targeted political campaigning is that these messages have a greater chance of going viral. This is achieved by sending the WhatsApp message directly to 500 people: 'there is no way that 20 per cent of those 500 persons would not push it to another person, saying *na read this o*, I just got this from WhatsApp, and that person would forward it to another person and before you know it, someone would send it to you without knowing that you are the one that generated it.'[29]

Despite these advantages, there remained some limitations to the use of WhatsApp for political campaigns in Nigeria. The first was that WhatsApp is not designed as a mass communication tool, and this limited its application during the 2019 presidential elections.

> I think you need to develop 'WhatsApp for politics' similar to the way you have the WhatsApp Business app. They need to allow a more mass usage of the tool … I think it is an under-tapped resource. One, because it gives you the opportunity to not only send message but audio-visual multimedia, pictures posters, campaign jingles. It would revolutionise campaigning. Because that way you are able to reach directly to the owner of the phone.[30]

Second, there are still many Nigerians who do not have access to the platform. With an estimated population of 208 million, Nigeria had 104 million internet users as of January 2021.[31] Even though messages shared on WhatsApp can penetrate and shape offline spaces,[32] this is hard to track for a campaign manager.

> Remember that WhatsApp is riding on android and data. You find out that behaviourally the greater percentage voting population who are traders are more incline to using what we call *kpalasa* phones [non-data driven phones].[33]

Handling falsehoods

Fake political messages or propaganda targeted at those seeking elected office in Nigeria is part and parcel of the campaign. False news and propaganda are tools used in the 'battle'[34] of Nigerian campaign noted one respondent, whilst another agreed that 'propaganda is part of politics, you expect it'.[35] But fake news on WhatsApp during political campaign has morphed into an art: 'it was literally easy to create, just the way people discovered and used this platform intuitively, they also discovered intuitively that fake news is a thing, and it became a thing, and it became a science and an art.'[36]

Whilst false news and political propaganda were noticeable in the 2015 elections, it reached a crescendo during the 2019 elections in the country due to what was described as an army of bad faith actors on all sides of the political divide:

> I know that both those sides did push out stuffs that was generally false, inflammatory and untrue. We saw it in 2015, bad faith actors won, I saw it in 2016 and they won. It is human nature when you don't penalise bad behaviour then society adopts it. You saw a lot more people on both sides using social media to push fake news to attack the reputation and integrity of candidates. And even then, there were still no penalties on either side. You sort of feel that you are going to see those types of inflammatory false propaganda campaign being pushed again by both sides in 2023.[37]

These messages tend to achieve their aim because of WhatsApp's high engagement rate and because people have more faith in the content shared on the application given that it often comes from a trusted contact or source.

> People were more able to interact with WhatsApp messages than they were to interact with a text message, we quickly found that one out. People are more likely to read it, respond to it or forward it.[38]

> Even if it is something as ridiculous as if you bath with salt at midnight, it will protect you from Ebola, because it is someone you know that is sharing that information people accept it at face value.[39]

To combat fake news targeted at their political principals, campaign managers set up social media units to dismiss allegations or rumours circulating online. An example of how this works was given in relation to the 2021 governorship election in Anambra.

> There was a day I came to one WhatsApp group. That morning Ifeanyi Uba [participant's rival] smartly injected one lie about a particular road, that he was the one that built the road. Of all the things he was saying, I left all those things and went to him and said 'Sir this one was done by Chris Azubogu" [the participant's candidate]. People wanted to close it and I said no! He [Uba] said what! Do I have evidence? He [Uba] released a document trying to prove that he built the road and the document messed them up. The document was addressed to a non-existing office and non-existing official. Because as of the time they wrote that letter, there was nothing like Ministry of Works, Housing and Power. The letter was dated October 2020. But the Ministry of Works, Housing and Power ceased to exist in 2019, Buhari has separated the ministry and moved the power away. So, there was no Minister in that name![40]

Others noted that 'whenever we receive such [a false] WhatsApp broadcast, we quickly fact check, respond and then rebroadcast. But you know they say, a lie goes round the world while the truth is still pulling its boot on'.[41] There was general agreement that you should not linger on trying to prove something was false. 'After the rebuttal move on,'[42] noted one respondent whilst another agreed that 'as a matter of strategy, once you respond, move to the positive things about your principal'.[43] But whilst political actors talked about the other side amplifying false information or how they respond to it, they never admitted to creating it. This is usually a missing part of the conversation about social media–mediated fake news propagation. Therefore, it is contentious to state that Nigerian political parties do not create fake news,[44] because their members and supporters propagate mis/disinformation,[45] either directly or by proxy, even if this is difficult to prove conclusively.

A new method of campaigning?

The 2019 vote was the second election in which WhatsApp played a significant role in political campaigning. But as findings from this study reveal, there was a gradual, but steady, rise of WhatsApp as a game changer for political campaigns in Nigeria from the 2015 election onwards. WhatsApp was deliberately and systematically employed by the political actors interviewed not only to target their audience but, above all, to make their messages go viral. The adoption of different WhatsApp groups, identification of primary and secondary carriers and, above all, targeting large WhatsApp groups where the political messages of their campaigns are amplified was seen as key in making the messages have impact.

Media and campaign officials sent direct and personalized political messages to voters, who ramped up the reach by making these messages go viral, thereby getting them to reach more people. This massive adaptation of WhatsApp, with a sophisticated campaign broadcast chain, has since become the norm in Nigerian elections.[46] This equally validates one of the propositions of the U&G theory, that users adopt the media that satisfies their convenience and utility needs.[47] In this case, social media campaign managers, having seen the inherent advantages in using WhatsApp for political campaign in 2015, used it again in 2019.

The systematic use of social media centres in 2019 shows a paradigm shift in digital communications as integral aspect of election campaigning in Nigeria. It is revealing that the campaign and media aides mechanically trail the messages of their principals by adopting various WhatsApp groups, creating a chain of broadcasting channels, in the process. They also dedicate time to monitoring content to either champion those in support or attempt to shut down those against their campaign messages. The period of the day in which these messages are pushed out is also very important. WhatsApp political campaign messages usually perform better if they are sent out 'early [in the] morning and late [in the] evening'.[48] For obvious reasons, people check their WhatsApp messages early in the morning before setting out for work and the same process occurs later in the evening when they are back from work.

But as the influence of WhatsApp has risen in elections and political campaigns in Nigeria, so too has its impact on propaganda and fake news. Findings suggest that the mis/disinformation was propagated by WhatsApp during the 2015 general elections. However, the influence of 'bad faith actors',[49] which became increasingly evident during the 2016 and 2017 governorship elections in Edo and Anambra states, reached a crescendo during the 2019 general elections.

One example of fake news was a video that widely circulated on WhatsApp before it was further amplified by a Twitter influencer. The video apparently showed an Independent National Electoral Commission (INEC) official thumb-printing ballot papers during the February 2019 elections for incumbent Muhammadu Buhari of the All Progressives Congress (APC). Investigations by International Centre for Investigative Reporting revealed it was false. The video, taken in 2015, was of an INEC official rigging elections for the Accord Party in Aniocha local government area, Delta state in what was probably a governorship election.[50] But before this narrative was corrected, and if recipients of the falsehood even received the correction, the impact of the rumour, in terms of undermining the election commission's credibility, was already being felt. Whilst fake news is not limited to WhatsApp – other social media platforms were used as tools propagating mis/disinformation, ethnocentric hate and political propaganda before, during and in the aftermath of the 2019 general elections in Nigeria[51] – what makes the platform unique is the intimate nature of the application. Messages often came directly from trusted sources which make recipient more likely to believe them.

A still limited impact

This study validates other studies that describe WhatsApp as a double-edged sword in the very heart of Nigeria's digitally mediated political campaigns and elections.[52] WhatsApp has been influential in spreading greater awareness about the promises and ambitions of aspiring political candidates. As one respondent noted, 'WhatsApp as a platform has been very wonderful tool for us in pushing our content. Through WhatsApp we were able to sell the candidate as someone that Anambra can trust'.[53] And it can continue to do so in future elections. On the flip side, WhatsApp has been a propagator and enabler of fake news in past elections and will likely again be used to drive division across ethno-political lines in forthcoming polls in Nigeria.

But it is important not to overstate the impact WhatsApp can have on candidate selection and political campaigns in Nigeria. WhatsApp political campaigns did not aid candidates to clinch their party tickets in the elections between 2015 and 2019. Party primaries are conducted by accredited delegates from the various states, who elect the party flagbearer. Nigerian party delegates are not swayed by WhatsApp messages; 'the delegates are totally beholden to someone who helps them determine who to vote for.'[54] Members of the political party usually conduct primaries to elect their party flagbearer. The election umpire, INEC, provides for both direct and indirect methods of party primary elections. However, most Nigerian parties usually opt for the indirect method[55] which involves prior voting to select party delegates, who will then vote in a governorship or presidential party flagbearer election. However, these party delegates are beholden to their political godfather, who selects the delegates and chooses who these delegates vote for during party primaries.[56] In Nigeria to a great extent, general elections are not determined exclusively by the quality of the political campaign. Rather, it is the financial clout and the support of political gladiators that selects the winners of general elections.

Notwithstanding the fraud, intimidation and large-scale violence that has characterized elections in Nigeria. WhatsApp is growing in importance for political campaigning in Nigeria. But it remains subservient to existing methods of winning voters. In other words, WhatsApp can be employed to push a godfather's chosen candidate forward or used in organizing an effective vote-buying operation just as much as it can be used to threaten to disrupt the status quo or to deliver more accountability in election processes.

Notes

1   Taye Babaleye, Pius Ibitoye and Emokiniovo Akpobo Odorume. 'Influence of social media on democratic governance in Nigeria'. *International Journal of Media, Journalism and Mass Communications* 6, 1 (2020), pp. 13–20.

2   Michael Aleyomi and Olanrewaju Ajakaiye. 'The impact of social media on citizens' mobilization and participation in Nigeria's 2011 General Elections'. *Centerpoint Journal* 17, 2 (2014), pp. 31–52.

3   Abdulmutallib Abubakar. 'Political participation and discourse in social media during the 2011 presidential electioneering'. *The Nigerian Journal of Communication* 10, 1 (2012), pp. 96–116.

4   Mala Mustapha. 'The 2015 general elections in Nigeria: New media, party politics and the political economy of voting'. *Review of African Political Economy* 44, 152 (2017), pp. 312–21.

5   Ripples Nigeria 2015. '2015 elections tear NLC apart', 12 February. Available at https://www.ripplesnigeria.com/2015-elections-tear-nlc-apart/

6   Lambe Kayode Mustapha and Bahiyah Omar. 'Do social media matter? Examining social media use and youths' political participation during . the 2019 Nigerian general elections'. *The Round Table* 109, 4 (2020), pp. 441–57.

7   Bello Shehu, Isa Inuwa-Dutse and Reiko Heckel. 'Social media campaign strategies: Analysis of the 2019 Nigerian elections'. Sixth International Conference on Social Networks Analysis, Management and Security 2019, pp. 142–49.

8   Obiriri Destiny Apuke and Bahiyah Omar. 'Fake news proliferation in Nigeria: Consequences, motivations, and prevention through awareness strategies'. *Humanities & Social Sciences Reviews* 8, 2 (2020), pp. 318–27.

9   Nwachukwu Egbunike. 2019. 'Twitter was a landmine of false information during the 2019 elections'. *Global Voices* 8 November. Available at https://globalvoices.org/2019/11/08/twitter-was-a-minefield-of-false-information-during-the-2019-nigerian-elections/

10   Farid Shirazi. 'Social media and the social movements in the Middle East and North Africa: A critical discourse analysis'. *Information Technology & People* 26, 1 (2013), pp. 28–49.

11   Christopher Akor. 'From subalterns to independent actors? Youth, social media and the fuel subsidy protests of January 2012 in Nigeria'. *Africa Development* 42, 2 (2017), pp. 107–27.

12   Nwachukwu Egbunike and Anthony Olorunnisola. 'Social media, igniting or damping the Nigerian Harmattan storm?' *Journal of Africa Media Studies* 7, 2 (2015), pp. 141–64.

13   See Global Voices. 'Global Voices special coverage — #EndSARS: A youth movement to end police brutality in Nigeria'. *Global Voices* (2020). Available at https://globalvoices.org/special/endsars-protest-nigeria-2020/; Oluwadara Abimbade, Phillip Olayoku and Dani Herro. 'Millennial activism within Nigerian Twitterscape: From mobilization to social action of #ENDSARS protest'. *SSRN* (2021).

14   See Egbunike and Olorunnisola. 'Social media, igniting or damping the Nigerian Harmattan storm?'; Bello et al. 'Social media campaign strategies'; Global Voices. 'Global Voices Special Coverage.'; U. Ojedokun, Y. Ogunleye, and A. Aderinto. 'Mass mobilization for police accountability: The case of Nigeria's #EndSARS protest'. *Policing: A Journal of Policy and Practice* 15, 3 (2021), pp. 1894–903; Oluwadara et al.

Millennial activism within Nigerian Twitterscape; Apuke and Omar. 'Fake news proliferation in Nigeria'; and Ebuka Igwebuike and Lily Chimuanya. 'Legitimating falsehood in social media: A discourse analysis of political fake news'. *Discourse & Communication* 15, 1 (2021), pp. 42–58.

15 Laura West. 'Facebook sharing: A sociolinguistic analysis of computer-mediated storytelling'. *Discourse, Context & Media* 2, 1 (2013), pp. 1–13.

16 Ruth Page. 'Re-examining narrativity: Small stories in status updates'. *Text & Talk* 30, 4 (2010), pp. 423–44.

17 Nic Cheeseman, Jonathan Fisher, Idayat Hassan and Jamie Hitchen. 'Social media disruption: Nigeria's WhatsApp politics'. *Journal of Democracy* 31, 3 (2020), pp. 145–59.

18 Elihu Katz, Jay Blumler and M. Gurevitch. 'Uses and Gratifications Research'. *The Public Opinion Quarterly* 37, 4 (Winter, 1973–1974), pp. 509–23.

19 See Jacques Richard Froget, Abbas Ghanbari Baghestan and Yasha Sazmand Asfaranjan. 'A uses and gratification perspective on social media usage and online marketing'. *Middle-East Journal of Scientific Research* 15, 1 (2013), pp. 134–45; Aysen Temel Eginli and Neslihan Ozmelek Tas. 'Interpersonal communication in social networking sites: An investigation in the framework of uses and gratification theory'. *Online Journal of Communication and Media Technologies* 8, 2 (2018), pp. 81–104; Xiaodan Liu, Qingfei Min and Shengnan Han. 'Understanding users' continuous content contribution behaviours on microblogs: An integrated perspective of uses and gratification theory and social influence theory'. *Behaviour & Information Technology* 39, no. 5 (2020), pp. 525–43.

20 Chukwuka Okonkwo (male, Igbo, lives in Lagos) volunteered for the Osita Chidoka 2017 Anambra state governorship campaign organization: Dupe Killia (female, Yoruba, lives in Lagos), was the national mobilizer and regional active volunteer management coordinator for the South West for a political party during the 2015 general elections: Ikechukwu Onyia (male, Igbo, lives in Abuja) worked in the media team of the following election campaigns: the Tambuwal 2015 presidential campaign, the Goodluck Jonathan 2015 presidential campaign, the Atiku Abubakar 2019 presidential campaign and the Chris Azubogu 2019 Anambra state governorship campaign: Ilemona Onoja (male, Igala, lives in Abuja), spokesperson for the 2019 Bola Saraki presidential campaign.

When Saraki was appointed Director General of the Atiku Abubakar Presidential Campaign, Ilemona became the DG's personal spokesperson: Ose Anenih (male, Esan, lives in Abuja), member of the 2019 Atiku presidential campaign organization.

21 Greg Guest, Arwen Bunce and Laura Johnson. 'How many interviews are enough? An experiment with data saturation and variability'. *Field Methods* 18, 1 (2006), pp. 59–82.

22 Igor Pietkiewicz and Jonathan Smith. 'A practical guide to using Interpretative Phenomenological Analysis in qualitative research psychology'. *Psychological Journal* 20, 1 (2014), pp. 7–14.

23 Personal interview with Dupe Killia, 7 July 2021.

24 Personal interview with Ose Anenih, 13 July 2021.

25 Ibid.

26 Personal interview with Chukwuka Okonkwo, 14 July 2021.

27 Personal interview with Ilemona Onoja, 7 July 2021.

28 Personal interview with Ose Anenih, 13 July 2021.

29 Personal interview with Ikechukwu Onyia, 8 July 2021.

30 Personal interview with Ilemona Onoja, 7 July 2021.

31 Simon Kemp 2021. Digital 2021: Nigeria. *DataReportal*, 11 February. Available at https://datareportal.com/reports/digital-2021-nigeria

32 See Idayat Hassan and Jamie Hitchen. 2020. 'How hashtag activism moves offline in The Gambia'. Democracy in Africa. 29 September. Available at http://democracyinafrica.org/hashtag-activism-gambia/

33 Personal interview with Chukwuka Okonkwo, 14 July 2021.

34 Ibid.

35 Personal interview with Ikechukwu Onyia, 8 July 2021.

36 Personal interview with Dupe Killia, 7 July 2021.

37 Personal interview with Ose Anenih, 13 July 2021.

38 Personal interview with Ilemona Onoja, 7 July 2021.

39 Personal interview with Ose Anenih, 13 July 2021.

40 Personal interview with Ikechukwu Onyia, 8 July 2021.

41 Personal interview with Ilemona Onoja, 7 July 2021.

42 Personal interview with Chukwuka Okonkwo, 14 July 2021.

43 Personal interview with Ikechukwu Onyia, 8 July 2021.

44 Idayat Hassan and Jamie Hitchen. 2019. 'Nigeria's "propaganda secretaries". *Mail & Guardian*, 18 April. Available at https://mg.co.za/ article/2019-04-18-00-nigerias-propaganda-secretaries/

45 Nwachukwu Egbunike. 2019. 'Social media propelled ethnocentric disinformation and propaganda during the Nigerian elections'. *Global Voices*, 6 November. Available at https://globalvoices.org/2019/11/06/ social-media-propelled-ethnocentric-disinformation-and-propaganda- during-the-nigerian-elections/

46 Cheeseman, et al. 'Social media disruption', pp. 145–59.

47 Thomas Ruggiero. 'Uses and gratifications theory in the 21st century'. *Mass Communication and Society* 3, 1 (2000), pp. 3–37.

48 Personal interview with Ikechukwu Onyia, 8 July 2021.

49 Personal interview with Ose Anenih, 13 July 2021.

50 ICIR. 2019. 'Fact-checking social media influencers who shared fake news during Nigerian general elections'. International Centre for Investigative Reporting, 24 June. Available at https://www.icirnigeria.org/ fact-checking-social-media-influencers-who-shared-fake-news-during- nigerian-general-elections/

51 See Igwebuike and Chimuanya. 'Legitimating falsehood in social media'.; Apuke and Omar. 'Fake news proliferation in Nigeria'.

52 Tzion Jones. 2021. 'WhatsApp drives a double-edged sword through Nigerian democracy'. *Democratic Erosion*, 19 January. Available at https://www.democratic-erosion.com/2021/01/19/fact-checks-and- balances-whatsapp-drives-a-double-edged-sword-through-nigerian- democracy/

53 Personal interview with Ikechukwu Onyia, 8 July 2021.

54 Personal interview with Ilemona Onoja, 7 July 2021.

55 Independent National Electoral Commission. Regulation for the Conduct of Political Party Primaries, Section 12b, 24 October 2014.

56 See Iwu Nnaoma Hyacinth. 'Party primaries and the quest for accountability in governance in Nigeria'. *Canadian Social Science* 17, 1 (2020), pp. 30–7; Isaac Olawale Albert. 'Explaining "godfathersim" in Nigerian politics'. *African Sociological Review* 9, 2 (2005), pp. 79–105.

4

Tailored to fit? WhatsApp marketing in Nigeria's fashion industry

Kolawole Talabi

Over a decade ago during the second year of my undergraduate studies as a geography major, I launched a side gig on my university campus. Through the benevolence of an aunt who had emigrated to London in search of greener pastures decades earlier, I became a part-time merchant of men's clothing – mostly British brands such as Burberry, Marks & Spencer and Primark. She would scout for sales during the retail off-season and send me clothing items that I would trade at budget prices while still making a handsome profit. Once I had sold a considerable portion of the consignment, I would send back the capital to the UK and the cycle would repeat itself. At the beginning, I was fortunate to have colleagues and roommates who, through word of mouth, brought in prospective patronage from among their own circles. Among my customers were professionals, students and tenured faculty members. Later, I decided to spread my entrepreneurial tentacles through direct marketing by commissioning low-end adverts.

Although I could not afford glossy prints, sales went through the roof. I got calls from prospective customers during lectures and study hours. As a student, it felt good having extra funds in the bank. At that time, only a fraction of students had smartphones. Non-touch display feature phones were already ubiquitous in the Nigerian market following the liberalization and deregulation of the telecommunications sector by the new democratically elected administration led by Olusegun

Kolawole Talabi is a media practitioner whose focus is on culture, digital and science stories. He is a food and wine specialist and life fellow of the Nigerian Conservation Foundation.

Obasanjo at the turn of the twenty-first century. But back then, I would have needed access to a huge database of telephone numbers to benefit from the latitude that text messaging offers. Fast-forward two decades, Nigerian entrepreneurs and small business owners are increasingly using smartphones to reach customers at home and even abroad through WhatsApp, the preferred messaging application of many Nigerians.

Besides the regular channels for exchanging information such as text, graphics, audio and video, two WhatsApp features have proved to be essential business communication tools for small and medium-scale enterprises and sole proprietors in Nigeria: the display picture and status update. Both have been commandeered by users for digital marketing purposes. Lacking the big budget that registered companies have for adverts and public relations, petty traders and small businesses are leveraging the immanence of WhatsApp as a communication tool to market products and services. Tailors, artisans, chefs, vendors, merchants and even farmers advertise their wares by changing the photo or video on the display picture and status updates on their WhatsApp accounts.

Unlike traditional media platforms such as print or radio, WhatsApp allows its users to measure metrics such as the number of people who see their status updates and by doing so, users can easily determine which posts work, and which do not. For users who seek to target more customers directly, WhatsApp Business offers additional marketing possibilities. WhatsApp and other social media platforms have transformed the marketplace. After the introduction of mobile phones shrank the distance between entrepreneurs and their clientele, the spread of internet technologies has expanded the channels through which market interactions can occur.

Where the market goes, the seller follows

On 22 February 2021, I sent a text message to *@ThatAdireGirl* to inquire about the purchase of Adire. Adire is the signature attire of the Egba people of Abeokuta – a bustling city situated in the wooded savannah of Yorubaland – about eighty kilometres from Lagos, Nigeria's busiest seaport and financial hub. Adire, which means 'tie and dye', is a material designed with wax-resistance methods that will produce patterned designs in a dazzling array of tints and hues. *@ThatAdireGirl* is an artisan textile venture being run by a working mother on Instagram and Twitter; two social media channels popular with younger and tech-savvy Nigerians. Her business started by accident on Twitter a decade ago in response to an urgent need for Adire which she had seen on her timeline. Sensing an opportunity, she half-jokingly tweeted, 'If I start selling adire, would you people buy?' It was a sales stunt: two days after the tweet, she made ₦40,000 – roughly US$80. The funds provided her with the initial capital to launch the business. Despite holding two university degrees in microbiology and a secure position in the state civil service, her interest in her 'side hustle' has not lessened.

In responding to my initial text, she first asked me to share my WhatsApp number. For many Nigerians, WhatsApp is an affordable means of communication. The text message I sent cost me four naira, but with as little as ₦1,000 – roughly US$2 – one can purchase over a gigabyte of data on most mobile networks in Nigeria, affording subscribers more value – voice and video – for price. She would later send me several designs from which I chose two classic designs. She then uses WhatsApp to share her design sketches. The platform also offers a space to negotiate prices and arrange for delivery logistics, which can be important in contexts where formal addresses are uncommon. Its importance to her business approach is exemplified by the fact that the profile section of her social media pages directs prospective buyers to her WhatsApp account. This use of WhatsApp for business communication is very common among Nigerian vendors, small businesses and sole proprietorships especially within the country's undercounted informal economy in which transactions worth several trillions of naira are done via unofficial channels each year.[1]

But in an effort to clamp down on illicit transactions and criminal syndicates, the Nigerian government recently mandated the linkage of all registered GSM telephone accounts to a national identity number, a set of eleven digits assigned to Nigerian citizens and legal residents by the National Identification Management Commission. After decades of failure in creating a centralized database for identifying its citizens, Nigeria is gradually trying to create a digital biodata repository for its almost 200 million people, but reaching those operating in informal spaces has proved difficult. At the end of the third quarter of 2021, just over fifty-four million persons had been registered in the national database. The multiplicity of identification numbers – Nigeria lacks a harmonized identity regime – has proved too cumbersome for Nigerians who operate in the informal economy. To improve enrolment rates, the federal government announced punitive measures; a directive to disengage the mobile telephone accounts of those who err to complete the enrolment exercise. However, this has never been carried out. Sole entrepreneurs or small businesses like @*ThatAdireGirl* who depend on WhatsApp for business communications cannot afford to have their lines disengaged. But that is not the only issue they have to worry about.

In 2021, WhatsApp informed the world of its plans to update the service's terms and privacy policy. On its website, WhatsApp said, 'we are making changes to our Terms of Service and Privacy Policy that relate to messaging between businesses and their customers on WhatsApp. We are also providing more information about how we collect, share, and use data.'[2] In response to public outcry on privacy concerns, WhatsApp subsequently clarified its policy, 'Your acceptance of the new Terms of Service does not expand WhatsApp's ability to share user data with its parent company Facebook.'[3] @*ThatAdireGirl*, who does not operate her own website, is not concerned about the WhatsApp updates because she has only maintained a messenger account rather than a business account.

Launched in 2018, WhatsApp Business is a free-to-download application that was built with the small business owner in mind. The application makes it easier to personally connect with customers, highlight products and services, and answer client questions. It allows for the creation of a catalogue to showcase products and services and uses special tools to automate, sort and quickly respond to messages. Although the basic version of WhatsApp lacks the accoutrements of the business version, @*ThatAdireGirl* has masterfully commandeered some of its features for marketing purposes. During her 2021 Easter clearance, she used WhatsApp status updates to advertise stocks in her inventory. The status allows users to share text, photo, video and GIF updates that disappear after a day. But there is a caveat to its utility and versatility for direct marketing purposes. To send and receive status updates to and from your contacts, you and your contacts must have each other's phone numbers saved in your phones' address books. This means that the larger the number of contacts in one's mobile address book, the greater the potential reach of one's status updates.

Finding fashion

Nigeria's fashion industry has witnessed a remarkable transformation in the last decade. The Lagos Fashion and Design Week was inaugurated in 2011 and it has been held annually, attracting entrepreneurs, exponents, exhibitors and enthusiasts. It has equally enabled Nigerian brands to attain international respectability. Luxury labels like ATAFO, Femi Handbags, Okunoren and House of Deola have already gained market leadership in West Africa and are working hard to put Nigeria on the world's fashion map. Unlike these bigger Nigerian brands, who can afford to do product placements or operate glossy websites staffed by media managers, emerging fashion entrepreneurs with limited marketing budgets must rely on the ubiquity of WhatsApp, the messenger and business accounts alike, to attract new clientele and retain old customers.

Charles Adebiyi is an engineer-turned-couturier who operates his outlet from Akure, a university town of rocky outcrops surrounded by dense rainforest in Nigeria's southwest region. He has always wanted to work in the fashion industry since high school, although circumstances beyond his control pushed him to study materials and metallurgical engineering at the federal university in Akure. But the engineering course exposed him to different materials: metals, ceramics, composites and polymers. When he understood that polymers are widely utilized in the textile industry, the knowledge reignited his adolescent passion for fashion. But fabrics are quite expensive in Nigeria. The collapse of the domestic textile industry means materials need to be imported from abroad. He got around this initial obstacle by sewing old bedsheets together for dummy attires which he posted on Facebook in a marketing stunt. It became an instant hit on social media as orders poured in from different sources. He steadily grew his customer base, and started charging the prevailing market price for his tailoring work, attracting clients both at home and abroad.

Charles operates a WhatsApp Business account that has a 'vendor' icon add-on which, when clicked on, loads a catalogue that showcases his array of fashion products. The catalogue displays a 'cart' icon add-on which allows prospective customers to ask about buying, customizing, delivery or anything they want. For now, businesses and customers who use WhatsApp Business in Nigeria are unable to process payments within the application, the service is available in India, with plans for a global roll-out. This follows an October 2020 announcement in which WhatsApp indicated it has plans to incorporate payments into the messaging application which will 'expand ways for people to check out available products and make purchases right from a chat'.[4] Charles switched to WhatsApp Business in January 2018, the month in which the latter was launched in Nigeria. 'When it came out, it didn't have [a] catalogue for multiple pictures,' he recalled of the oldest version of the WhatsApp Business app. 'It was upgraded with time, with more features.'[5]

After relocating abroad, Charles had to change telephone numbers, but that has not stopped him from using his old WhatsApp Business account that is linked to a Nigerian number. This is perhaps one of the biggest advantages of the private messaging application. Its universality enables users to continue using a WhatsApp account even when they no longer reside in the dialling code domain where they opened the account. It is therefore not unusual for small business operators to have more than one WhatsApp account. Many of the dominant smartphones in the Nigerian market also come with WhatsApp pre-installed which further explains its ubiquitous adoption by users.

Charles's current catalogue on his WhatsApp Business account contains four photos: one of a female model sporting a chef's attire, a red men's shirt and the remaining – two white T-shirts made with cotton embroidered with Kente fabrics – a material that is native to Ghana, and two full-length Kente trousers. Charles's sartorial designs have been sold both locally and overseas to Nigerian expatriates and immigrants – a student in Malaysia as well as residents of Ohio and Wisconsin in the United States. He charges between ₦5,000 (US$10) for a Kente T-shirt and ₦35,000 (US$70) for business suits. Native casuals, like Kaftan, cost ₦10,000 apiece (US$20). But despite his digital business operations, Charles still has had to deal with offline structures such as Nigeria's state-owned postal colossus, well known for its bureaucratic tardiness and operational inefficiencies, to ship packages. A reminder that despite the vast range of digital tools for selling the products and services, business owners still must navigate the many challenges posed by doing business in Nigeria's offline realm. In its 2020 Doing Business index, the World Bank Group ranked Nigeria 131 out of 190 countries, up fifteen spots up from its position in the previous yearly ranking, but still indicative of an environment where obstacles to doing business exist.[6]

WhatsApp business communities

Building on Nigeria's strong tradition of labour unions,[7] which dates back to 1912 when the Nigeria Civil Service Union was formed, WhatsApp groups are engendering supportive online communities. The Christian Designers Hub (CDH), which uses WhatsApp extensively to engage its members, is one of these social communities created specifically for professional tailors. The CDH attracts top fashion designers and graphic artists. Its members must pay an annual subscription fee of ₦10,000 – roughly US$20 – to participate in the group's activities or organized meetings. The Hub also operates a corporate account with the international freight giant DHL. This strategic partnership enables all its members to send products and deliver services to different parts of the world at a discounted price. Other benefits include in-person workshops and training sessions, field trips and company excursions, middlemen referrals and advertisement placements on the Hub's website.

The Hub operates four WhatsApp groups to engender camaraderie among its teeming membership of fashion entrepreneurs and design specialists whose devotion to God is unabashedly expressed. Charles, who joined about three years ago, says the support members get from the group is great. He values the *esprit de corps* that CDH provides. He recounted how one of the group's inspiring voices, Ugo Monye, found professional success and industry recognition when Ebuka Obi-Uchendu, a former contestant and current host of popular reality TV show *Big Brother Naija*, sported an Agbada he made and posted it on Instagram. By sharing these success stories, up-and-coming members who are struggling to gain a foothold in the sector get an emotional boost and the chance to learn first-hand from accomplished industry veterans.

WhatsApp groups have evolved to become a functional crucible in which individuals with shared goals or entities with common interests come together for community-building exercises in all sectors of life in Nigeria. Due to the volume of its membership, the Hub's four WhatsApp groups have dedicated administrative support. Members get business tips, and Q&A sessions on strictly fashion-related matters are encouraged. Besides these topics, only motivational stories and faith-based experiences are permitted. CDH's convener, Femi Odusoga, says that, despite the Hub's Christian leanings, it is open to people of all faiths even those without any religious affiliation as long as they abide by the group's values and beliefs. Femi Odusoga counts at least four Muslims among its members. The Hub teems with aspiring designers and established names whose contributions have uplifted the group's *esprit de corps*, especially founders who have mastered the use of various digital marketing channels to advance their commercial interests amidst Nigeria's difficult business climate. The Nigerian government has not demonstrated public support for online transactions. In fact, its high-handed policy on cryptocurrencies, digital wallets, capital controls and the recent seven-month ban imposed on Twitter are examples of how Nigeria stifles e-commerce and web-based businesses.[8]

For many Nigerian entrepreneurs who are already burdened by the difficulty of doing business in the country, any free-to-download application that helps business operations is a welcome development in their already challenging occupational environment. Gbenga Enikanosaye, the owner of a clothing label that is part of a bigger fashion company, registered his business with the relevant authority upon completing his industrial traineeship a decade ago, but he laments government's inability to support small enterprises. 'I have never gotten any assistance from my local government… the truth is, they don't even have a database of entrepreneurs. So, there's no way they can render assistance [because] they don't know who is who.'[9] His need for community however led him to apply for the Hub's membership two years ago. The application process is straightforward: a basic registration plus the fees. Gbenga gained more than just camaraderie from his membership. He admitted that one of the workshops on fashion photography really transformed his thinking. In 2020, he began using WhatsApp Business which brought in more than thirty orders. He does WhatsApp stories too, reaching hundreds of viewers per time: 'the annual due we pay for CDH membership is nothing compared to what we gain from the WhatsApp groups. Information is power.'[10]

Ruth Ogbeide, the founder of Bloomkids, is braving the rigor of running a venture in Nigeria's economic omphalos, Lagos. Building on the boom for proudly Nigerian products between 2014 and 2016 she launched a children's clothing line five years ago. But Ruth says poor urban planning, and a lack of customer parking, in the Ikeja precinct of Lagos where her flagship store is located impacts on sales. Once leafy and kempt as Ikoyi, the doyen demesne of Nigeria's erstwhile federal capital, the Ikeja of today is a built-up zone of polluting industrial estates, mega shopping malls, glam tech cynosures, overpriced luxury apartments sprawling residential neighbourhoods, pharaonic public buildings, endless dual carriageways, obstructive traffic circles, high-rise commercial towers, kilometres of street lights interspersed by resplendent outdoor advertising, red-light bazaars, a big civilian aviation facility – Murtala Muhammed International Airport, and of course – a restless phalange of human faces and forms.

To offset this hurdle, she resorted to online search engine optimization and linked her address to the company website. The website's homepage contains a WhatsApp Business click-to-chat feature that simplifies the overall shopping experience, facilitating a premium customer experience for intending clientele. Bloomkids website operates a digital trolley in which shoppers can create a wish list, add products to a cart, checkout and make payments. The WhatsApp Business feature on the website provides extra customer engagement and support in addition to email, tweets, frequently asked questions and newsletters. 'I do my marketing on WhatsApp. ... since the advent of WhatsApp Business, it draws people closer than the other channels.'[11]

Tope Williams-Adewunmi is a board member of the CDH. She regularly delivers Instagram TV webinars on how to use WhatsApp Business, an example of the growing overlap of social media and private messenger applications. In one short but crisp video she created recently, Tope euphoniously directed a graphic step-by-step guide that detailed her experience with the different features and toolkits of the application. She commenced by displaying her WhatsApp Business profile and provided soundbites to accompany the changing images in the graphic tutorials adeptly. She discussed the app's various add-ons-cum-features and their corresponding usefulness, setting up the business profile, and how to use the catalogue manager. Thereafter, she explained how to use the application's different messaging features such as 'away message' which is used to reply automatically when you're away, 'greeting message' for welcoming new customers automatically, 'quick replies' for repetitive messages, and lastly, 'labels' for organizing chats and customers into neat categories.

Martwayne, a training outfit for aspiring designers who want to start a fashion house, is the brainchild of Williams-Adewunmi. From its Lagos offices, Martwayne conducts its operations by organizing physical instruction for fashion students. But increasingly additional online courses have been created for people who prefer distance learning. During Covid-19 restrictions, courses were only available online. A quick look at her catalogue reveals a snippet of her ambitions. Offerings included two e-books and some instructional manuals – sewing classes for kids (which cost ₦15,000 for the DIY option and ₦30,000, around US$60 for the premium one) and an online course in sewing and patternmaking with fees starting at US$0.70 per day for a certificate. A second course, *Sewing Techniques for Perfect Finishing* targets 'anyone who wants to learn how to operate a serger for a clean finish'. The course grants enrollees a twelve-week unfettered access to tutorials that cost US$0.17 per day. These are budget rates compared to what obtains at legacy fashion institutes. First-year tuition (plus academic supplies) for the 2021/2022 academic session at Fedisa is around US$7,100. This explains why most aspiring fashion designers opt for less pricey in-house apprenticeships. Martwayne provides this more affordable approach, but with an extra moxie – the chance to learn at your convenience using digital technologies as a pedagogic medium.

A business and cultural lifeline?

In December 2021, the Nigerian Communications Commission (NCC) in collaboration with the Ministry of Communications and Digital Economy organized an auction for the country's 5G broadband service with three bidders competing for the two available slots.[12] This is a welcome development as the technology is expected to fast-track the growth of Nigeria's digital economy, open more business opportunities for entrepreneurs and grow the stagnant economy. It has also been critical in helping many Nigerians survive, economically, the Covid-19 pandemic.

The onset of Covid-19 which led to civilian lockdowns in Nigeria, and forced local firms and international organizations to mandate remote work, fast-tracked the adoption of teleconferencing software for some operations and most meetings. Whilst it disrupted the fashion industry in many ways, it also opened new opportunities for growth. The facemask, which quickly became symbolic of the coronavirus pandemic, has become a new item for individuals to sell. For small businesses and entrepreneurs, WhatsApp has been a lifesaver during the pandemic. It has enabled fashion designers to continue to accept and process orders without having to meet clientele. Ruth Ogbeide introduced kerbside delivery options for her Afrocentric children's clothing line in Lagos that she manages using the application. Furthermore, the feelings of loneliness which the prolonged social distancing and sheltering protocols engendered during the recurrent civilian lockdowns of the coronavirus pandemic made memberships of occupational WhatsApp groups like CDH more common.

In a low-trust society like Nigeria, the personal touch that WhatsApp offers is essential in building trust between sellers and their potential customers. Fraud is a big issue in online transactions, and people are wary of businesses without physical outlets. Besides obtaining the telephone number of a prospect, the ability to take screenshots of chats between users offer an additional level of trust that may turn a random business query into sales. In doing so, WhatsApp is doing a lot to bridge Nigeria's long-standing digital and economic divide between its educated elite and their compatriots who do not possess the same level of institutional credentials. 'I will say the majority of Nigerians using a smartphone will use WhatsApp,' Osazua Iruedo, a business manager, commented in a Quora post in response to the question, 'How many Nigerians use WhatsApp?'[13] Her response also noted how it enables conversation and is easy to use for people with a little knowledge of technology.

Notes

1 Joseph Tonuchi and Peter Idowu. 'How large is the size of Nigeria's informal economy? A mimic approach'. *International Journal of Economics, Commerce and Management* 8, 7 (2020), pp. 204–28.

2   WhatsApp. 'We are updating our Terms of Service and Privacy Policy'. Available at https://faq.whatsapp.com/general/security-and-privacy/were-updating-our-terms-and-privacy-policy?ref-banner

3   WhatsApp. 'Terms of Service and Privacy Policy'.

4   WhatsApp Blog. 2020. 'Shopping, payments and customer service on WhatsApp'. 22 October. Available at https://blog.whatsapp.com/shopping-payments-and-customer-service-on-whatsapp/?lang=en

5   Author's interview with Charles Adebiyi, 17 April 2021.

6   World Bank. 'Doing Business Report 2020'. World Bank (2020).

7   Ade Ademola. 'The History of Trade Unionism in Nigeria'. *Ind-Africana: Collected Research Papers on Africa* 2, 2 (1989) pp. 13–30.

8   Daniel Adeyemi. 2021. 'Nigerian businesses face an avalanche of losses as the Twitter ban continues.' *Tech Cabal*. 25 June. Available at https://techcabal.com/2021/06/25/nigerian-businesses-face-an-avalanche-of-losses-as-the-twitter-ban-continues/

9   Author's interview with Gbenga Enikanosaye, 2 May 2021.

10   Ibid.

11   Author's interview with Ruth Ogbeide, 1 May 2021.

12   Nigeria Communications Commission. 2021. '5G: Mafab, MTN Emerge Winners in Nigeria's 3.5GHz Spectrum Auction.' Available at https://www.ncc.gov.ng/media-centre/news-headlines/1137-5g-mafab-mtn-emerge-winners-in-nigeria-s-3-5ghz-spectrum-auction

13   Osazua Iruedo. 2018. 'How many Nigerians use WhatsApp'. Quora. Available at https://www.quora.com/How-many-Nigerians-use-WhatsApp

5

'The Forum': A WhatsApp support group for health and social service providers during the Anglophone crisis in Cameroon

Kamila Pacholek, Madalina Prostean, Sarah Burris, Lynn Cockburn, Julius Nganji, Anya Nadege and Louis Mbibeh

Amidst the ongoing Anglophone crisis in Cameroon, a WhatsApp group called 'The Forum' was created in March 2019. The Forum brought together forty-five diverse individuals, mostly from Cameroon, to support knowledge sharing and skill acquisition in mental health and trauma-informed care. In doing so it created a virtual community of practice, highlighting one way in which WhatsApp can be used to facilitate connection, support and knowledge-sharing among practitioners, even in difficult contexts.

A community of practice is a professional group in which members share common professional interests and enhance their knowledge through ongoing interaction. There is evidence to support the efficacy of communities of practice generally[1] and more specifically, virtual communities of practice for health and social service providers.[2] One additional documented benefits of virtual communities of practice include the ability to connect geographically dispersed professionals, allowing knowledge sharing in challenging contexts, with lesser constraints on space and time.[3]

Kamila Pacholek, Madalina Prostean, Sarah Burris, Lynn Cockburn and Julius Nganji were with the Department of Occupational Science and Occupational Therapy, University of Toronto, Canada at the time of writing this chapter.

Anya Nadege Independent Researcher, Kumba, Cameroon.

Louis Mbibeh works at the University of Bamenda, Bamenda, Cameroon.

This chapter will explore the experiences of Forum participants, Forum coordinators and researchers to share what was learned from these experiences. It offers unique individual and team perspectives on facilitating a community of practice using WhatsApp, how practitioners learned by being involved in a WhatsApp group, and reflects on how WhatsApp can facilitate community-based research in a West African setting.

The Anglophone crisis

Cameroon has been governed by one ruling party which has had power since independence in 1960 and 1961, with only two presidents since then. The current president, Paul Biya, has been overseeing the country for four decades since first taking office in 1982. Since 2016, the North West (NWR) and South West (SWR) regions of Cameroon have been affected by armed conflict.[4] In Cameroon, about 80 per cent of people are Francophones while the rest – most of whom reside in the NWR and SWR – speak English. The roots of what has come to be known as the 'Anglophone conflict' extend back decades and include several interwoven factors. Underpinning these are the impacts of colonization by German, French and British, on all sectors of life, including legal, business, development, education and religious sectors.[5]

As a result of the colonial project, Cameroon officially has both French and English as national languages, and citizens are expected to be bilingual. But both state and individual bilingualism are elusive.[6] While it is unknown how many citizens have verbal fluency in both languages, many people estimate that the actual numbers are low. Of the more than 200 indigenous languages, none is officially recognized for education or government business. With the rise of English on the global scene, many Francophone elites send their children to English language schools.

Understanding the complex nature of the practical implications of the ten administrative regions in the country is beyond the scope of this chapter. However, a major concern for many in the two Anglophone regions has been the gradual increase in French language policy, use, and practices in these regions. Examples include teachers who were placed in English schools but could not speak English and required students to sit exams in French, and lawyers who were placed in positions which used English common law but who were trained in, and came to their posts expecting to use, French civil law.[7] For years, peaceful appeals and complaints had been made, requesting the government to recognize these shortcomings and make appropriate changes, but with little impact.

In 2016, in response to the marginalization and underrepresentation by the central government, many English-speaking Cameroonians in the NWR and SWR began to organize peaceful mass protests. These actions provoked immediate and violent responses by government forces. With escalating state-sanctioned violence, some citizens began to fight back. The conflict, which continues at the time of writing this chapter, has caused at least half a million people to flee their homes, and has led to thousands of civilian casualties, kidnappings, bombings and the burning of buildings.[8] Violence has been perpetrated by the government, military and separatist forces, and has led to forced closures of many schools and hospitals.[9]

Health services have been significantly impacted by the conflict. Hospitals and health centres, as well as health and humanitarian workers, have been the target of violent attacks while at work and in communities.[10] An already fragile and poorly resourced health system has felt the pains of even more difficulties because of the attacks, the losses in revenues and the flight of many healthcare providers to other parts of the country. In 2020, the Covid-19 pandemic added significant stress to the health system.

Individuals with disabilities have been badly affected by the conflict, targeted by both separatist and government forces as they struggle to evacuate unstable areas, or are left behind.[11] In their attempts to gain control and to silence dissent, the government has also shut down the internet connection several times in the

Anglophone regions without warning. One of the longest blackouts lasted 240 days in 2017.[12] Even when the internet connection is enabled, the service remains costly and unstable, challenging a vital resource for communication and interpersonal connection. One GB of data costs around US$1 a day, less if purchased in larger amounts. For the average worker, a monthly salary is between US$100–$200 (CFA50,000–100,000). Compounding this difficulty, many people had reductions in income and increased poverty as a result of the conflict.[13] The cost of living has continually increased and access to electricity and internet became more and more difficult. By 2021, it was common that many days only saw a few hours each week of electricity and internet access.[14]

As a result of the conflict, healthcare workers in these regions face increased challenges in providing services to clients. Health and social service provision was made more difficult because of pre-existing and compounded limitations in resources, social isolation and stressful environments.[15] Most of the healthcare services focused on supports for physical interventions, and there was little training for dealing with the trauma that was emerging in communities.

> People, including all of us working in health care, are living in fear, not sleeping well due to gunshots at any time, can't remember specific things, can't trust others, feeling depressed – the number of people needing mental health services in the NWR has increased dramatically.[16]

The impact of the conflict on mental health has been immense, with both clients and professionals at risk of psychological trauma. As a result, an increased demand for mental health and trauma-informed care has often outweighed providers' capacities and levels of expertise. The risk of trauma, coupled with an increased need for mental healthcare, made it difficult for service providers to meet the needs of the patients and clients, as well as their family and friends. Many have been struggling to meet their own personal care needs along with the needs of their colleagues.[17]

The Forum

A group of healthcare providers set out to collaborate and provide a way to support people who experienced trauma and mental distress. As these leaders discussed strategies that could be implemented, one identified aim was to create a group that would bring people together to try to support each other. They chose WhatsApp because it was familiar and easy for people to use on their mobile phones. Many of the health professionals who requested support did not have regular access to computers or electricity, and in-person meetings were not an option due to the insecurity.

The Forum was piloted in 2018. Initially, the group ran for a few weeks to see if it could be effective, and if members wanted to participate. There were positive responses. It was formally launched in March 2019. For the first six months it ran with a carefully constructed agenda. Since then, The Forum has continued to operate, with some formal topics and much informal discussion.

The Forum's main aim was to provide professional support and education on mental health and trauma-informed care to healthcare and service providers practicing in the context of the Anglophone crisis. The goal was initially to primarily support providers in the NWR and The Forum was set up as a private WhatsApp group with approximately forty-five participants. Most of The Forum members were based in Cameroon, while some living outside of the NWR and the country joined in support of their colleagues. The Forum allowed them to connect virtually as many had been physically displaced.

One part-time coordinator helped to keep the activities on track, with several volunteer coordinators participating in the group. The coordination group had a separate WhatsApp group that they used to plan, monitor and evaluate the group's activities. These WhatsApp administrative coordinators vetted potential participants, often had one to one conversations with group members to answer personal questions and received suggestions. The coordinators maintained a list of participants, added them to the WhatsApp group and, in the first year of the group, made daily postings to start conversations or raise topics for discussion. Guidelines and expectations were conveyed during the first few weeks of the group meetings. Individual follow-up happened as needed.

The coordination group discussed their experiences with other WhatsApp groups, and collaboratively developed rules for participating in the group (see Table 1).

When The Forum started, the coordinators made the plans explicit. Recognizing that many members were living in a conflict zone with

Table 1 Ten general rules for discussions on The Forum WhatsApp group

1. Daily Greetings should be limited to Hi/Hello.
2. Please focus on supporting others, and the topic at hand. **No posting of religious information, games, graphic pictures, political party advocacy, or adverts during the discussions.**
3. **For personal discussions**, individually connect with the person concerned. If you are not sure how to do this, ask one of the Admins.
4. Please read others' comments before posting yours.
5. Stick to information that is relevant for the day's discussion.
6. Double check your write up before posting.
7. **Respect confidentiality**, conceal clients/patients names and other identifying information. Don't share people's posts outside of the group. Documents and resources can be shared.
8. You are free to post whenever you are able within the day and as little or as much as possible.
9. Indicate clearly which conversation you are responding to if possible. If you are not familiar with the reply option for a message, please ask someone to show you.
10. We want to have a safe and supportive forum. Respect each other in your comments and in case you feel you are hurt or angered by a comment get to the group admin immediately for his or her support and response, rather than to fight back.

Source: The Forum.

insecurity and unpredictability, were members of other WhatsApp groups and were also working full-time jobs in healthcare, it was important to be sensitive to not overload them with information. The information plan that the coordinators developed at the beginning is provided in Table 2.

Each month there was a theme. Weekly, a specific topic was facilitated by designated members. For example, in the second week the discussions focused on the services and resources which were available

Table 2 Orientation message

So, a big WELCOME! please suggest others who might be interested. We will be in touch with the specifics. The content will be similar to the first week in the Pilot Project, but each week will have a topic, rather than each day. One topic will be spread out over the week. We are also aware that because of the situation, many of you will be deleting messages. That is understood.

Day 1
1) Welcome message, requesting for introductions
2) Provision of Forum Guidelines
3) Pause for introductions to start
4) Topic 1: It starts with us: Taking care of ourselves

Day 2
1) Revised welcome message – 'Welcome to Day 2'
2) Re-Post of guidelines – Guidelines were posted every morning for Week 1, and then weekly after week one and when needed
3) Keeping a log – Discussions about how people could track the information they were gathering.
4) Topic 2: Managing stress

Days 3–5
1) Revised welcome message – Welcome to Day 3, 4 and 5
2) Repost Guidelines each day
3) Continue introductions as needed and continue conversations

---

Source: The Forum.

in the NWR, since many people had expressed concerns that it was very difficult to find services that met the needs of their clients. One post in The Forum during the second week was:

> **Week two: Resources available in the NWR to support our clients and ourselves.** *Last week we were discussing on how to take care of ourselves in times of trauma. We thank everyone who shared thoughts and ideas on how to take care of ourselves. If you still have some strategies on self-care you want to share in the course of the week, please feel free to do so. This week we shall be discussing on the resources available in the NWR to provide support to people that are traumatized. There is need for services and resources that can easily be accessible to provide support in times of trauma.*
>
> *What are some resources available in the NWR that provide support to people affected by the crisis?*

In response, members posted specific contact information for a range of services. The coordinators clarified details with those who had posted information, confirmed that the responses were correct and compiled them into a resource list that was shared back with the group members.

The coordinators used their own understandings of the situation and received suggestions from members to develop a plan for what would be discussed. Table 3 lists the topics of each month with some comments about the focus of each week's discussions.

Table 3 Plan for six months of The Forum

Month	Topic	Focus of weekly discussions
		Note: The last week of each month focused on a recap of the month and evaluation
March	Welcome and getting started	Ground rules and guidelines
		Introductions of members
		Overview of the six-month program

Month	Topic	Focus of weekly discussions
		Note: The last week of each month focused on a recap of the month and evaluation
April	Understanding trauma and trauma informed services	What is trauma? and how it affects people
		The basic principles of trauma informed care
		Interventions that are most useful in conflict situations
		Reference manual: Trauma informed principles through a culturally specific lens by Josie Serrata and Heidi Notario
May	Strategies for interventions	Basics of REBT, Rational Emotive Behaviour Therapy, for African contexts
		The use of expressive therapies in conflict situations and to cope with trauma
		Introduction to working with children, children's mental health, how trauma affects children
June	Focus on children and trauma	Discussion of ways that the forum helped members to understand the experiences that children were going through, and the supports and services that were available
July	Continuing the discussion, No formal topics	Members continued to share information about trauma, stress, and possible interventions
August	Conferences Wrap up	Sharing of information learned from various conferences that members had attended
		Formal end of the six-month programme

Source: The authors compiled this table using information about The Forum.

Research about The Forum and WhatsApp use

As the group unfolded, it was agreed by the coordinators that doing some formal research on it would be beneficial. In 2020, a research project to explore and document the range of experiences in greater detail was conducted. The project aimed to learn about the ways in which health and social service providers used The Forum in their everyday lives and professional practices, to cope with the immense tragedy and trauma happening around them.

Data for the research was collected through online semi-structured interviews, relying on an interview guide with questions and prompts, which could be modified depending on each individual conversation.[18] This interview style allowed for a balance between consistency and flexibility, which was important for ensuring participants were able to share their individual perspectives. Information about the research was posted on The Forum group, and interested members were encouraged to reach out if they wanted to participate. To maintain confidentiality with the group itself, we did not research any of the actual WhatsApp discussions or share information about who was in the group.[19]

A total of thirteen participants took part in the study: ten living in Cameroon and three living in North America (two having recently moved from Cameroon). While not all participants had training in mental healthcare, approximately 85 per cent did, with all reporting frequent contact with clients in their respective fields. In their work, participants used various therapeutic approaches, including counselling, motivational interviewing, cognitive behavioural therapy and psychoeducation. Participants in the study shared the weight of their experiences, telling stories about violence, fear and the challenges of working in a conflict zone.

The team transcribed the interviews and then coded them in accordance with Braun and Clarke's outline of data analysis.[20] First, we familiarized ourselves with the data, generated initial codes and created a code book. Next, codes were grouped into categories, and we created themes representative of the data overall. In this sense, codes can be understood as the raw data points while themes are generated from our analysis. Throughout the process of analysing data and documenting results, the diversity of the research team was highly beneficial.[21] Team members with direct lived experience of the Cameroonian conflict were able to provide insight unavailable to the Canada-based researchers, allowing for a more nuanced understanding of the data set.

WhatsApp as an effective platform

The study determined that WhatsApp is an effective platform to host a virtual community of practice. Several WhatsApp features, including its relative ease of use, made it well suited to this purpose. The majority of participants already employed the application in their everyday lives for personal and group communications. WhatsApp also allowed for flexibility, as participants were able to search keywords and scroll through previous posts to re-read content, even when offline. This was particularly important for members of The Forum who were in conflict regions subject to unstable internet connection and internet blackouts. As one participant noted.

> Oh, [what] helped me the most to connect with others was just the WhatsApp [...] I cannot pay for phone calls, because phone calls are expensive. So the WhatsApp was really helpful.[22]

The format of WhatsApp allowed for members to participate in ways that they were comfortable with, as people already had the application loaded on their phones. From previous experiences, most knew how to post and respond, whilst some members needed additional coaching to understand how to use some of the features available in WhatsApp. For example, when responding to a post, it can be helpful to include the original post in the response; some participants were initially not aware that they could link the original post to the response and indicate exactly what they were replying to. This was particularly important when there were several threads of a conversation happening on the same day or week, and people would be coming in and out of the conversations at different times. Some members also needed training on how to format messages to include bolding, emojis and line breaks.

Several members actively participated by frequently posting, commenting or posing questions to the group. Many were quieter, posting infrequently or for a few, not at all. Through the research interviews, it emerged clearly that several members felt involved by reading and considering the information, even if they did not respond to it in the group. It was also apparent that in addition to individual preferences, contributions were impacted by the unreliable internet or phone capabilities of many members. Silence, therefore, proved to be extremely complex, and influenced by a multitude of factors:

> I am more into listening than talking… which will translate to more reading than sharing. However, for me personally, I've come to learn that sharing is also a healing aspect to the person sharing. So, I would understand that for those who chose not to participate, not to contribute, they had reasons why.[23]

WhatsApp was also seen to be affordable, an extremely important consideration in areas where poverty rates and the cost of living are both high. Finally, the internal, end-to-end encryption used within WhatsApp meant that members had some assurance that messages were not usually being shared. However, many members were still cautious, as they knew that messages could easily be forwarded out of The Forum group without permission, despite the requirement to maintain confidentiality in the established group rules.

Clinical utility and application to practice

The challenges of delivering health, and especially mental health services amidst the conflict, increased the prevalence of traumatic experiences for both providers and clients. Participants discussed the increased need for trauma-informed care across health and social service settings – even those members that were not directly providing mental health services. Participants also discussed the limited opportunities to engage in professional learning groups, particularly around mental health.

As indicated in Table 3 (see page 95), there were facilitated topics each week for the first six months. At the beginning of each week, the person who was facilitating for the week would provide some information and resources. Often the facilitator would also provide questions aimed to start discussion or to elicit stories from members. For example, in Week two, the resource about trauma was used to shape specific, key points about trauma informed care. Only a few discussion points were shared at one time to prevent members from feeling overwhelmed by posts, and the follow-up responses.

In The Forum, members had the opportunity to share information, discuss challenging client cases and ask questions. The group was diverse in clinical experiences, and users learned from one another regardless of their level of expertise. Through WhatsApp, this professional community was made less restrictive, and more accessible and interactive than traditional educational settings, providing opportunity for candid discussion and professional networking. Participants recognized how the virtual space was informal but effective, as reflected in the following quotes.

> The forum for me is a virtual space where professionals from the field of mental health can share their own experiences. Because they're usually left out as we tend to forget they also require opportunities to talk about their challenges.[24]

> To me, the Forum was a platform where practitioners in the field of mental health and some branches of medicine participated on a daily basis, to improve their services on the field. For me personally, it was a place of inspiration. A place where I could do referrals, and also get information on some certain issues.[25]

While there was no pressure for everyone to contribute, the coordinators did encourage members to make comments. The research revealed that both coordinators and members would reach out individually to members at times when it was felt that it might be helpful. For example, members who had very similar areas of practice might have a private side conversation to talk about their experiences, or a coordinator or other member might reach out privately at times that a member posted something especially sad or difficult, for example, witnessing gunfire or hearing of the death of children due to combat, to offer personal support.

Participants appreciated the professional resources offered and frequently saved content from The Forum for later use. WhatsApp allows the saving of various file formats with relative ease, especially for those who have higher end phones. Videos, pictures, MS Word and PDF documents, and audio recordings were all shared to assist members in understanding the concepts under discussion. As a result of the ongoing conflict there has been very few training or professional development opportunities in the NWR. The members often expressed appreciation for access to current resources and to people who could answer specific practice-related questions.

All members of The Forum attempted to keep the focus on practical information that would assist the group members in their day-to-day work. Stories about specific situations were shared, with concern for confidentiality. The stories would lead to comments and suggestions from others, and often the original poster reported gratitude.

> Some of the participants, they will put active case studies [in The Forum] – case studies that are real. And they will ask in The Forum to everybody what they can do, and from those exchanges we are able to bring up ideas and suggestions as to what, [or] how they could handle those situations as therapists.[26]

Several participants stated that they were able to apply what they learned in The Forum to their professional practice. As one participant noted, 'the direction of every discussion was triggered by real needs of health care workers or patients. All the time, the discussions were helping us meet needs.'[27]

Social support

The WhatsApp platform allowed members of The Forum to connect across time and geographical locations. This was of particular benefit for the group as participants were able to read posts and reply in their own time zone, without missing out on discussion. Results of our study showed that The Forum provided members with social support that went beyond the professional nature of the group. In The Forum, members provided one another with encouragement, a listening ear and strategies for self-care. The need for self-care was especially important in the context of their work, with most participants commenting on the importance of understanding that 'if you don't care for yourself, you can't help others'.[28]

Members also emphasized how important it was for them to be among peers, noting that sharing experiences was affirming. Support was offered to each other, in small but important ways, such as sharing morning greetings, and larger ways, such as talking about personal and emotional care for front-line workers.

> Yeah, I can't really remember who did the post, but it was about self care.. I would just feel burned out. I was feeling burned out, but people need help, I just keep going, going, going, going, and at one point I felt I was going to break down. And I can remember someone saying, if we don't take care of ourselves, we, we have to take care of ourselves in order to take care of others. And that those words took me aback. I sat for a moment, and I reflected and reflected, and there were times that I needed to slow down. I then tried to watch on my own health, my own mental health, so that I can continue to be strong for them. Because if I crack down and they are cracking down, then nobody can help anybody in that situation. So when I feel like I'm getting to the edge, I just need to slow down and take care of myself, so then I can keep going. Yeah, I really reflect on that.[29]

As the quote above indicated, members shared messages with each other, in attempts to boost morale in the extremely difficult circumstances. There was discussion in The Forum conversations about how important their work was, and that they needed to take care of themselves so that they could continue to care for others. Members were encouraged by hearing stories of how others were going through similar experiences as they were, or even just that there were people in The Forum who cared about them.

> I've been living in a crisis region and… to just know that you have another professional who thinks about you, who can support you, who can just give you a tap on your back, encouraging you.[30]

This participant talked about how The Forum provided a unique, and safe, online space to connect and debrief after a difficult day.

> Just knowing someone is thinking about you, helps you a lot in this situation. You get up to go to work and there [are] gunshots and you have to hide… But by the time you come back, if there is internet and somebody [asks] you 'How are you today? What is happening?', and maybe you share a bit… and somebody encourages you, it is a big plus because they are maintaining that balance.[31]

For example, one member who did not have formal mental health or trauma training stated:

> One thing I remember very well is the suggestion from one member… that we could reduce or avoid listening to, or watching, stress-building images of killings or destruction of property. Because of that, I deleted several images from social media and blocked some contacts and groups on social media. That helped me.[32]

From the beginning of the conflict, a downside of the use of social media and private messenger applications such as WhatsApp was the ease of sharing unfiltered images. Especially in the first year or two of the conflict, the sharing of horrific images, such as images of military abuse of young students, or dead bodies, with no warning was a regular occurrence. A person could be in the middle of doing any ordinary daily activity, open an image and suddenly see an extremely disturbing image, sometimes of someone they knew or even a family member. While the impacts of this in The Forum are unknown, the negative psychological impacts of increased exposure to explicit, violent images on social media have been demonstrated, for example, from France[33] and the United States.[34] WhatsApp group administrators in communities of practice groups and healthcare-related groups need to be aware of their responsibilities and liabilities related to this kind of sharing.[35]

However, the social aspect of the group went beyond that of support. In the crisis context, participants were able to use The Forum to check in with others regarding their safety and well-being. Seeing posts from colleagues who were living in active conflict zones where thousands of people were being displaced from their homes, experiencing kidnappings and attacks on hospitals could mean that the person was surviving and managing to keep going. This was relevant for members both in and outside of the conflict region. One member described using the WhatsApp group to keep tabs on close friends and colleagues who were living in Cameroon, as checking the group, and seeing that someone they knew had posted recently, offered some measure of relief.

Replicating the model

It can be challenging to maintain professional guidelines on WhatsApp, as it is used for multiple purposes by different groups, often for informal and casual conversations. One way of maintaining a professional space is to have a coordinating group responsible for setting and maintaining group norms and guidelines for conduct. The Forum had four coordinating members, who initiated the programme and except for one (who received a small honorarium), volunteered their time. Members appreciated their efforts to keep the group running smoothly. The research participants clarified that the benefits of having coordinators included setting of clear guidelines for professional interaction, establishing discussion topics, monitoring the pace of discussion and encouraging members of The Forum to participate and contribute.

Many participants in The Forum discussed their limited professional development and expressed a desire to diversify their professional interactions. Members enjoyed interactions with those from different professional disciplines, practice settings, and geographic locations, as this brought unique perspectives and dynamic discussions. There was also diversity in levels of experience with mental health and trauma-informed care, as well as the number of years in practice. This diversity allowed less experienced practitioners to learn from expert sources, while also providing opportunities for those with more experience to practice and tailor their teaching style for this varied audience.

Over the past few years, there have been other reports supporting this kind of professional benefit for health professionals, and other groups. Examples include Woods et al[36] who documented the use of WhatsApp among medical doctors in South Africa; Alanzi et al.[37] who used WhatsApp for patient education about diabetes, and McIntyre and Sobel,[38] who reported on the impacts of WhatsApp groups among Rwandan journalists. There are also many other undocumented groups that have been developed and continue to emerge.

But there remain concerns that learning in a WhatsApp group might not be as comprehensive as when other strategies are used. For example, Clavier et al.[39] found that medical residents who received information via WhatsApp were more satisfied than those who received it through traditional email formats, but their clinical reasoning was worse. They speculated that one reason might be the divided attention apparent when accessing information through a smartphone.

Nonetheless, WhatsApp appears to offer strategies for enabling diverse and dispersed professionals to interact in meaningful ways, overcoming barriers imposed by time and location. For anyone interested in developing a virtual interactive learning community, expanding membership to include individuals from a variety of professions, settings and geographic locations, with varying levels of experience, can have significant benefits. But in these interactive and diverse learning communities, there are various nuances of which the organizers should be aware. Two factors that emerged from our research which may also have an impact in other WhatsApp-based communities are the range and types of WhatsApp groups that members belong to (WhatsApp 'cultures') and their associated roles; and the meaning of silence.

Most Cameroonians belong to many types of WhatsApp groups – family, social, professional, faith-based and so on. The type of group influences the level of one's involvement and activity, and members often naturally take on certain roles based on their experience and participation in other groups. Being aware of these dynamics is vital when it comes to assigning certain roles in a group or letting them be decided on organically, setting norms around participation, or even pre-screening members for their intended level of participation. We are also informally starting to hear of what might be called WhatsApp group fatigue, as what was a novelty a few years ago (when The Forum started) seems to be growing and becoming more commonplace; many people in our networks report being members of twenty-five, fifty or more WhatsApp groups. It can be extremely difficult to maintain currency and enthusiasm in all of them.

The importance of not taking silence in the discussion personally was another important learning from the study. When, at times, participants did not or could not respond to the discussions, both facilitators and members could feel discouraged or frustrated. Several respondents made comments that indicated an understanding of the belief that when group members did not respond messages, it was not necessarily because they did not want to. There was recognition that some people were limited from responding to messages or discussions because of poor network or the cost of accessing the platform. Such silence is understandable, as most of the participants in Cameroon lived in the turbulent NWR and were generally cautious about what they posted to social media. Even in closed WhatsApp groups, messages can be forwarded with attribution to a particular person (sometimes wrongly), without permission and out of context. Many people either had these kinds of negative experiences or knew of others who had. Some research participants even stated that there have been instances of people being attacked in their homes because of statements made online in social media though we were not able to find documented evidence to support these claims. As a result, many members preferred to read posts, but not participate in discussions.

Privacy, trust and security were crucial to members of The Forum, as participation in this group was risky. By engaging in The Forum, members risked unknown consequences if military personnel or rebel group members found information shared on the group by its participants that they deemed problematic. An example of this caution was that The Forum was originally called the Crisis Support Forum, but the name was shortened in response to group members' safety concerns and a request that the word 'crisis' not be used in discussions because of the political connotations. For those who would like to create a WhatsApp group that aims to serve as a virtual place of learning being aware of these factors and learning about the context of members' lives can help manage expectations and bolster participation.

This chapter has examined how WhatsApp was used in the everyday lives of healthcare and social services practitioners living through the ongoing political conflict in Cameroon. The Forum has shown that practitioners can engage meaningfully on WhatsApp in a way that helped them cope with personal, work and societal challenges, while assisting them to provide services. The ease of use of WhatsApp even promoted support and community beyond that of a professional nature.

At the time of publication, the WhatsApp group remains open and continues to function as both a source of information and support for practitioners.[40] Membership has grown in numbers as well as in diversity. The Forum can therefore serve as blueprint for clinicians, practitioners, educators and researchers, who wish to engage in similar pursuits in Cameroon and in the region more widely.

Notes

1   Angie Hart, Ceri Davies, Kim Aumann, Etienne Wenger, Kay Aranda, Becky Heaver and David Wolff. 'Mobilising Knowledge in Community-University Partnerships: What Does a Community of Practice Approach Contribute?' *Contemporary Social Science* 8, 3 (2013), pp. 278–91; Glibert Probst and Stefano Borzillo. 'Why Communities of Practice Succeed and Why They Fail.' *European Management Journal* 26, 5 (2008), pp. 335–47.

2   Stephen Barnett, Sandra C Jones, Sue Bennett, Don Iverson and Andrew Bonney. 'General Practice Training and Virtual Communities of Practice – a Review of the Literature.' *BMC Family Practice* 13, 1 (2012), pp. 87–87; Lynn Cockburn, Louis Mbibeh and Jacques Chirac Awa. 'The GRID Network: A Community of Practice for Disability Inclusive Development.' *Disability, CBR & Inclusive Development* 30, 2 (4 October 2019), pp. 84–94.

3   Hermon Ogbamichael and Stuart Warden. 'Information and Knowledge Sharing within Virtual Communities of Practice.' *South African Journal of Information Management* 20, 1 (2018), pp. 1–11.

4   Human Rights Watch. 2020. 'Cameroon: Events of 2020.' Human Rights Watch, 18 December. Available at https://www.hrw.org/world-report/2021/country-chapters/cameroon

5   Eric Anchimbe. 'The Roots of the Anglophone Problem: Language and Politics in Cameroon.' *Current History* 117, 799 (2018), pp. 169–74.

6   Nguh Fon. 'Official Bilingualism in Cameroon: An Endangered Policy?' *African Studies Quarterly*, Black Studies Center 18, 2 (2019).

7   Anchimbe. 'The Roots of the Anglophone Problem: Language and Politics in Cameroon'; International Crisis Group. 2017. 'Cameroon's Worsening Anglophone Crisis Calls for Strong Measures.' International Crisis Group, 19 October. Available at https://www.crisisgroup.org/africa/central-africa/cameroon/130-cameroon-worsening-anglophone-crisis-calls-strong-measures.

8   OCHA. 2021. 'Cameroon Situation Report.' 3 June. Available at https://reliefweb.int/country/cmr; Cameroon Anglophone Crisis: Database of Atrocities. Available at https://research.rotman.utoronto.ca/Cameroon/PressRelease.html; Siobhan O'Grady. 2019. 'Cameroon's Crackdown on Its English-Speaking Minority Is Fuelling Support for a Secessionist Movement.' *Washington Post*, 5 February.

9   International Crisis Group. 2020. 'Easing Cameroon's Ethno-Political
      Tensions, On and Offline.' International Crisis Group, 3 December.
      Available at https://www.crisisgroup.org/africa/central-africa/
      cameroon/295-easing-cameroons-ethno-political-tensions-and-offline
      & O'Grady. 'Cameroon's Crackdown on Its English-Speaking Minority Is
      Fuelling Support for a Secessionist Movement.'

10   Moki Kindzeka. 2018. 'Medical Staff Targeted in Cameroon's English-
      Speaking Regions'. *Deutchse Welle*. 17 August. Available at https://www.
      dw.com/en/medical-staff-targeted-in-cameroons-english-speaking-
      regions/a–45119170

11   Alphonse Tebeck. 2020. 'Challenges Faced by Cameroonians Living with
      Disabilities Aggravated by Anglophone Crisis.' *Radio France International*,
      14 November. Available at https://www.rfi.fr/en/africa/20201114-
      challenges-faced-by-cameroonians-living-with-disabilities-aggravated-
      by-anglophone-crisis.

12   Thijmen Calis. 2018. 'Cameroon Shuts down the Internet for 240 Days.'
      Tech Tribes. 29 August. Available at https://techtribes.org/cameroon-
      shuts-down-the-internet-for-240-days/

13   OCHA, 'Cameroon Situation Report'.

14   Aboudi Ottou. 2021. 'Power Outage, Debts, Dilapidated Electricity
      Transport Infrastructure: ENEO's CEO Opens up about the Problems
      Facing the Cameroonian Electricity Sector'. *Business in Cameroon*.
      19 April. Available at https://www.businessincameroon.com/
      economy/1904-11472-power-outage-debts-dilapidated-electricity-
      transport-infrastructure-eneo-s-ceo-opens-up-about-the-problems-
      facing-the-cameroonian-electricity-sector

15   Alice Debarre. 'Providing Healthcare in Armed Conflict.' International
      Peace Institute. December 2018. Available at https://www.ipinst.org/wp-
      content/uploads/2018/12/1812_Hard-to-Reach.pdf

16   Author's interview with participant. 6 March 2020.

17   Moki Kindzeka. 2018. 'Cameroon Doctors Ask for Protection as Attacks
      by COVID Carriers Increase.' *Voice of America*. 18 May. Available at
      https://www.voanews.com/africa/cameroon-doctors-ask-protection-
      attacks-covid-carriers-increase

18   Sharan B Merriam and Elizabeth J. Tisdell. *Qualitative Research: A Guide
      to Design and Implementation*. Electronic resource. Fourth edition. The

Jossey-Bass Higher and Adult Education Series (San Francisco, CA: John Wiley & Sons, 2015).

19 Sergio Barbosa and Stefania Milan. 'Do Not Harm in Private Chat Apps: Ethical Issues for Research on and with WhatsApp.' *Westminster Papers in Communication and Culture* 14, 1 (2019), pp. 49–65.

20 Virgina Braun and Victoria Clarke. 'Braun, Virginia; Clarke, Victoria. Using Thematic Analysis in Psychology.' *Qualitative Research in Psychology* 3, 2 (2006), pp. 77–101.

21 For this research three graduate students in occupational therapy were recruited and a research team was formed with the coordinators, an additional researcher and the students. The team benefitted from having both insiders and outsiders involved in the process.

22 Author's interview with participant. 6 March 2020.

23 Author's interview with participant. 26 February 2020.

24 Author's interview with participant. 2 April 2020.

25 Author's interview with participant. 24 May 2020.

26 Author's interview with participant. 6 March 2020.

27 Author's interview with participant. 9 April 2020.

28 Author's interview with participant. 2 April 2020.

29 Author's interview with participant. 24 May 2020.

30 Author's interview with participant. 12 March 2020.

31 Ibid.

32 Author's interview with participant. 9 April 2020.

33 Robert Maelle et al. 'Media Exposure and Post-traumatic Stress Symptoms in the Wake of the November 2015 Paris Terrorist Attacks: A Population-Based Study in France'. *Frontiers in Psychiatry* 12, 524 (2021).

34 Alison Holman, Dana Garfin, Pauline Lubens and Roxane Cohen Silver. 'Media Exposure to Collective Trauma, Mental Health, and Functioning: Does It Matter What You See?' *Clinical Psychological Science* 8, 1 (2020), pp. 111–24.

35 Carolyn Bouter, Bonnie Venter and Harriet Etheredge. 'Guidelines for the use of WhatsApp groups in clinical settings in South Africa'. *South African Medical Journal* 110, 5 (2020), pp. 364–8.

36 Joana Woods, Michelle Moorhouse and Lucia Knight. 'A Descriptive Analysis of the Role of a WhatsApp Clinical Discussion Group as a Forum for Continuing Medical Education in the Management of

Complicated HIV and TB Clinical Cases in a Group of Doctors in the Eastern Cape, South Africa'. *Southern African Journal of HIV Medicine* 20, 1 (2019), pp. 1–9.

37   Turki Alanzi, Sulaiman Bah, Sara Alzahrani, Sirah Alshammari and Fatima Almunsef. 'Evaluation of a Mobile Social Networking Application for Improving Diabetes Type 2 Knowledge: An Intervention Study Using WhatsApp'. *Journal of Comparative Effectiveness Research* 7, 9 (2018), pp. 891–9.

38   Karen McIntyre and Meghan Sobel. 'How Rwandan Journalists Use WhatsApp to Advance Their Profession and Collaborate for the Good of Their Country'. *Digital Journalism* 7, 6 (2019), pp. 705–24.

39   Thomas Clavier, Julie Ramen, Bertrand Dureuil, Benoit Veber, Jean-Luc Hanouz, Hervé Dupont, Gilles Lebuffe, Emmanuel Besnier and Vincent Compere. 'Use of the Smartphone App WhatsApp as an E-Learning Method for Medical Residents: Multicenter Controlled Randomized Trial'. *JMIR MHealth and UHealth* 7, 4 (2019).

40   For more on The Forum see Sarah Burris, Kamila Pacholek, Madalina Prostean, Lynn Cockburn, Julius Tanyu Nganji, Nadege Anya and Louis Mbibeh. 'A WhatsApp Virtual Community of Practice: Mental Health Education and Support for Practitioners during the Anglophone Crisis in Cameroon'. *Disability and the Global South* 8, 2 (2021), pp. 2094–115; Kamila Pacholek, Madalina Prostean, Sarah Burris, Lynn Cockburn, Julius Nganji, Anya Ngo Nadège and Louis Mbibeh. 2021. 'A WhatsApp Community Forum for Improving Critical Thinking and Practice Skills of Mental Health Providers in a Conflict Zone'. *Interactive Learning Environments*, 5 March; Kamila Pacholek, Madalina Prostean, Sarah Burris, Lynn Cockburn, Julius Tanyu Nganji, Nadege Anya and Louis Mbibeh. 'WhatsApp as Occupation and Professional Development: The Example of Mental Health Education and Support for Practitioners during the Anglophone Crisis in Cameroon'. Ghana, 2020.

6

The dynamics of WhatsApp usage among elderly Nigerians

Temitayo Olofinlua

In 2020, as the world faced the Covid-19 pandemic, countries across the world grappled with a digital infodemic – an excessive spread of largely unreliable viral information about the virus – spreading from phone to phone. In Nigeria, much of this information moved through WhatsApp groups and message chains with significant blame apportioned to the elderly as leading proponents of 'forwarded as received' messages.[1] Media articles predominantly focus on the 'dark side' of the platform; however, there is more to the use of WhatsApp than misinformation. This was exemplified by a 2020 Nigeria Health Watch report[2] that examined how it was a platform for social mobilizing and networking online to reach the vulnerable in need of financial assistance. This shows that limiting the conversation on WhatsApp use to the 'dark' perspective reduces the space to examine the nuances of the conversations and networks being built among older people on the platform. In this chapter, I examine the day-to-day uses of WhatsApp by older Nigerians – individuals over sixty – how they exist in WhatsApp groups, and analyse some of the content disseminated on the private messaging application.

According to DataReportal, as of January 2021, there has been a 22 per cent increase in use of social media by Nigerians from the previous year with 'thirty-three million social media users ... equivalent to 15.8 per cent of the total population.'[3] Of these, WhatsApp is the most used; even though there are no specific statistics delineating WhatsApp use by different age groups in Nigeria, studies show that

Temitayo Olofinlua is a freelance writer, editor and researcher of digital spaces.

older adults have a high adoption rate when it comes to mobile phone use.[4] Despite this, technology adoption by younger demographics has been the focus of many WhatsApp studies to date. Ahad and Lim[5] examined the domestication of WhatsApp as a convenient means of communication among undergraduate students in Brunei. Previous studies on WhatsApp in Nigeria have also focused primarily on younger[6] and female users.[7] They have illustrated how WhatsApp was used for evidence gathering and information dissemination during the #EndSARS protests in Nigeria; by acting as a bridge between the predominantly young protesters and older Nigerians as the youth shared 'videos of their peaceful demonstrations and evidence of further harassment by the police across WhatsApp groups, to better inform a key demographic: older Nigerians'.[8] But insufficient attention has been given to studying how elderly users experience the application in Nigeria and what challenges they face when it comes to acting responsibly online.

Outside of Nigeria there have been a few more studies of mobile phone use among the elderly. Nair[9] examined how elderly people in Malaysia are becoming dependent on their mobile phones, especially after they overcome their initial fear of the technology. Similarly, Fernández-Ardèvol et al.[10] investigated how old people in a Canadian retirement home make use of mobile phones. They show how intertwined their relationship with different media technologies – television, newspapers, phones and more – is. From the study, the respondents indicate their need for particular media in five main ways:

> (1) Media are for maintaining connections with people with whom they have a deep prior relationship. (2) Mobile phones are important for being able to reach someone – and to be reached quickly – in case of an emergency. (3) These seniors engage in filtering different media in and out of their lives, depending on what they want to manage and what they think is an appropriate use of a particular media form for a particular type of communication. (4) They circumscribe their use of media by defining what amount of time they devote to it, or because of the extent of the networks they want to maintain. (5) Finally, the

octo and nonagenarians express forms of attachment to particular media, which influence their decisions about what is an appropriate communication device to use in particular circumstances.[11]

While enquiring how the elderly use mobile instant messaging (MIM), including WhatsApp, Kiat and Chen[12] found that the architecture of most of the platforms were not suited to the needs of the elderly, despite the ability of the application to support interactions. They noted that 'user interface design features such as small font size, confusing icons and application flow in current MIM applications, however, make them difficult for the elderly to learn and use'.[13] A Pew study further supported this claim, noting that older Americans face peculiar challenges, some of which are age-related health problems while others deal with a lack of confidence in their ability to use the devices as they are forced to rely on younger people to guide them on how to use the mobile phone. Despite this, once they can use the devices, they quickly become a part of their daily reality.[14] While this study applies to old people in America, a similar narrative exists with elderly Nigerians. With many of them retired, they have more time on their hands. As such, the mobile phone serves purposes beyond communication and access to information, with many users even dependent on their mobile phones,[15] and increasingly WhatsApp, for everyday life interactions.

For this chapter, I interviewed nine elderly regular WhatsApp users from southwest Nigeria, four men and five women, who were largely retirees from different occupations – teachers, broadcasters and business owners – and who live in urban areas.[16] This chapter provides insights into how the application 'behaves' in the hands of these retirees. It highlights six dimensions to WhatsApp use, for most of these respondents. First, continuing already existing conversations in the offline world on WhatsApp. Second, reclaiming lost connections. Third, accessing and sharing information with others. Fourth, as a tool to engage with the outside world or as a form of passing time, especially when bored. Fifth, many of them have some kinds of attachment to WhatsApp, in what can be categorized as fear of missing out. Finally, abuse of the platform, which happens because many of them are not informed that sending 'forwarded as received' messages is not responsible behaviour.

Everyday living online

Every morning when Victoria Olawoore, sixty, wakes up, she says her prayers. Then, she reaches for her phone and goes on WhatsApp. She gets into her family group – called Graced Ones – where she checks on all her children by sending a 'virtual good morning' which is often accompanied by prayers. This simulates what would happen if all the respondent family members were living together in the home. Just like all greetings, she expects a response. If she does not hear from any of her three children via WhatsApp, that is her cue to call the 'erring' child. After this, she checks and responds to any messages demanding her immediate attention – from friends and on groups that she belongs to – before continuing with the routine of the day. Olawoore's use of WhatsApp has become an integral element of her everyday living since she got a mobile phone in 2017, mimicking what she would have done previously without the application. Through WhatsApp, she simulates the reality of family co-habitation through their WhatsApp group, 'it is not the same, but it is what we have and make use of.'[17]

While such connections can also be continued on similar instant media messaging, or even social media platforms, Olawoore, as well as other respondents, says that WhatsApp is the preferred application because she can reach out to many people at once in privacy – in much the same way as you engage family members within the house. For instance, in the case of her family, through the group, she achieves the same purpose of checking on all of them at once because it is more affordable and helps with faster information dissemination:

It reduces costs of text messages and calls. If you want to send text messages to other people outside the country, it is more expensive. With WhatsApp, there are no extra costs for sending such messages. It has also made the costs of calls cheaper. It helps to spread news more than normal message. It also means that most of the messages are in one space. I search for the person and I am able to trace the messages easily, unlike on the mobile phone where I have to be searching, month by month. It is more convenient to use.[18]

Other respondents agreed that compared with the telephone charges, WhatsApp is cheaper and gives more value for money. Unlike the typical phone call charges – for instance one SMS costs ₦4 within Nigeria and as much as ₦20 to send internationally – once you have loaded your mobile phone with data, you are able to send several WhatsApp messages to many people. Rates vary but 200MB, which last for three days, costs ₦200. WhatsApp is cheaper but it has also made continuing connections with offline relationships online easier as respondents see their bigger community – of families, retirees, of landlords, old students, church groups, and more – reflected on the platform.

Beyond connection with their immediate families, users also find it a tool that makes it easy for them to re-establish connections with old friends. 2011 was the year Witemire, now seventy, retired, got a mobile phone and began to reconnect with her other retired colleagues through WhatsApp. No longer bound by the constraints of an 8am to 2pm job, the retired teacher now spends her time reconnecting with past colleagues and engaging in church activities on WhatsApp. For her, the platform is important in helping to rekindle existing relationships with her previous colleagues, especially because they no longer see each other daily. The platform also became a space for sharing any retiree-specific information:

> It was important because those were times when government would ask us to go for some verification exercises [about pensions]; without WhatsApp, it would have been harder to pass the information quickly. Through that we can know where to go, what to do, more easily.[19]

Beyond reconnecting with past colleagues, by belonging to groups like old students' associations, older users can also reconnect with past friends. Akinniran Alabi, sixty-one, says that WhatsApp has been an avenue for him to connect with old students from his alma mater where they bond over past events and are able to come together to also support their schools. A WhatsApp study by O'Hara et al. of users in the UK highlighted this:

> Participants' experiences in WhatsApp, appear bound up in the enactment of their day-to-day relationships... WhatsApp here is a site of encounter with these friends; a means by which, we would argue, they can exhibit small but frequent acts of commitment and faithfulness. It is part of the way these relationships are experienced and constructed as an ongoing matter; in essence, part of the way they live and dwell together even when apart.[20]

The retirees spoken to for this research are familiar with their WhatsApp friends' 'online daily rituals' to the extent that they can embed themselves into them. This suggests that it is also important that connections on WhatsApp build on ones that already exists, between people that already understand one another's daily lives. For instance, due to the time difference between Nigeria and America, Witemire calls her children, who are based in the United States, in the evenings. She also video-calls her grandchildren because she wants to see them; to see how well they look. Through these video calls, even though she cannot touch them, she can simulate reality because she can hear their voices and get a better sense of how they are. Consequently, though miles apart, she can be part of important moments in their lives, making WhatsApp 'a powerful life logging tool'.[21]

However, there are cases where WhatsApp also opened the door to people many of the respondents did not have an initial 'day-to-day relationship' with. For example, Alabi said that this has happened to him a couple of times with people sending him pornography or adding him into WhatsApp groups where people propositioned him with business ideas that requested his financial support:

> People have tried to defraud me via the platform. When I retired anew, people, many of them I did not know, thought I would get my gratuity

and they were bringing different offers. They were asking me to come and be involved in businesses. Some others, they will be flaunting some imaginary business ideas that they think you will like: fake customs people telling you to come and buy rice for ₦4,000 when it costs over ₦20,000, and even fake car deals. Several scam ideas asking me for my bank verification number. Most of them I delete them when I see them.[22]

Other respondents also received fraudulent messages when they were added to new groups of through voice calls. However, many of them are already aware of how these kinds of frauds manifest through phone calls and emails in Nigeria, meaning they are better equipped to detect them. Some of them also admitted to forwarding the messages to their children who subsequently warned them against sharing their bank details with anyone online.

A source of information

While all the respondents engaged with other forms of media such as newspapers, television and radio, WhatsApp still played an important role as a source of information. On WhatsApp, they garnered information that they would ordinarily not get through other media platforms. For instance, during the #EndSARS protests, which called for the disbandment of the Special Anti-Robbery Squad in Nigeria, information about the largely youth-driven movement was proscribed in traditional media. As such, young people engaged older people with information about the protests via WhatsApp, and used it to dispel misinformation.[23]

Asides from information that they received from person-to-person messages, older Nigerians also access information as group members. As previously established, many of the groups are tied to offline networks they already belong to – family, past work groups, religious groups, retiree and old students' associations. In religious groups – Witemire belongs to the Catholic Women Organisation in Akoko

South for example – they share information about church activities such as women association meetings and other upcoming events. For community groups like landlord association groups, which many respondents belonged to for their different communities, information is shared about community meetings and security issues. While alumni association and retiree groups are more groups for socializing and sharing information about retirement benefits.

Bayo Olujimi, a retired civil servant, belongs to over twenty groups on WhatsApp. Olujimi has a daily chore in each of these groups. He sends newspaper headlines to the different groups that he belongs to. He gets the newspapers from a group that he belongs to and shares with the retiree groups 'to get them informed, since most of them are no more in active public service'.[24] For someone like Olujimi, the platform is an avenue to disseminate information; he does this because he says that he is aware of the disconnect of many retirees from the current events in the society. Unlike before when they would go to their different workplaces and be intimated with 'gist' of ongoing events around them from their colleagues, this does not happen after retirement. This is why he shares messages on the platform on a daily basis: to keep other retirees informed of national events every morning, as it would have been if they were still in active service.

Olujimi's example raises questions about content moderation in a space where once you are added by someone as a contact, you cannot control the form of information shared with you. While accessing information may be beneficial, there are also challenges with information overload and the spread of 'fake news'. Akinniran Alabi complains of this: 'there are times when I leave the messages unread because they are too many. How many can I even read at once? So, I only try to quickly look through the messages to see what applies to me.'[25] On WhatsApp, the only way to control the deluge of information is to block a sender but only just over half of the respondents were aware this button existed.

For many retirees, WhatsApp is simply a time-filler which they use to engage themselves as many of them have retired from work and their children are gone to universities or are married. Siaka Kolapo Olawumi, sixty-two, can hardly do without his phone. Whatever he is doing, his phone is usually close by. Since he retired, even though he has filled his life with other activities including pastoral work, WhatsApp remains a constant fixture. Through the platform, he can stay informed allowing him to inform others and engage in debates. He says that once he starts scrolling through the messages, it is usually difficult for him to stop:

> There is always something to read; a message, a video to watch, a piece of information, something to learn. However, it is time consuming. You start and you don't want to stop. It is very very addictive. I am addicted to WhatsApp. Sometimes before I pray in the morning, I grab my phone because I want to see what has happened while I was asleep. You want to see what is happening. It is my main tool for getting information and being up-to-date with what is happening around.[26]

Even though he is an avid user of the platform, he also laments that there is a lot of fake news spreading on the application which he says he tries to avoid participating in, 'you cannot push anything to me and believe that I will spread it. I digest the information I receive and ask myself: can it be true? Is it true?'[27] He says that if he is unable to answer these questions, he refrains from sending it to others and even takes it upon himself to correct the sender. He does this by checking to see if it is from a reputable media source; 'many of them are not… some of the stories are just outright rumours that have been circulating around WhatsApp'.[28]

To check the spread of unverified news on its platform in 2020, Twitter introduced a warning notice whereby whenever a user is about to share information containing an external link on the platform, they are asked if they want to read the information before sharing. WhatsApp indicates when a message has been 'forwarded many times', but this is largely reactionary and more needs to be done by the platform to limit the spread of falsehoods.

The DTTC ERUWA '81 group

When some old students of the Divisional Teachers' Training College (DTTC), Eruwa, Oyo state, gathered to celebrate SK Olawumi's son's wedding, they began to think of ways to extend the camaraderie beyond the physical space. Since they left the school, they had all spent decades apart in their different lives. Many of the students had not seen each other in that time and they sought ways of continuing the reconnection, even after the wedding. That was how the group named DTTC ERUWA '81 was born on WhatsApp. The members of the group had passed through the institution between 1978 and 1981. Today, the WhatsApp group has over ninety-two members and is a beehive of activity and information sharing.

Most of the posts on the platform can be categorized into three main areas: the first is targeted information that contains specific information for the group members, usually about retirement benefits. Second are messages on specific themes like health, politics or religion. Third are messages with entertainment value. While the first category of information is usually specific and useful to the members of the group, the other types of information cannot be said to have a specific use, but they do have a notable structure.

On specific themes such as health, messages are crafted as if they are from authority figures such as medical doctors, academics or even pastors that readers would likely believe. Second, the messages are framed as if they have the interest of the reader at heart, making promises about the information can improve your health or avert falling ill. As such readers get interested by seeing the benefits of the message even if many are false or misattributed. Finally, many of the messages have a call to action, asking readers to do something, usually to forward to other people. Below is an example of a health-related message:[29]

> A Nigerian officer in the USA has sent this through to help each and everyone. Please read and take care of yourself, Dr Okyere.
>
> The rate at which young people are suffering from kidney disease is alarming I am sharing a post which can help us. Please read

below: IMPORTANT KIDNEY DESERVES THE BEST. Barely two years ago, we all received the news of the Nigerian actor as a result of kidney disease. ALSO OUR MINISTER OF PUBLIC WORKS, the Honourable Teko Lake is currently in the hospital on life support with kidney problems. I want to show you how to avert this menace of kidney disease.

SO HERE ARE THE TOP 6 CAUSES OF KIDNEY DISEASE: 1. Delaying going to the toilet... 2. Eating too much salt... 3. Eating too much meat... 4. Drinking too much caffeine... 5. Not drinking water... 6. Late treatment... Please before deleting, please help your friends by passing it. It might help someone. Pass to as many as you can. WhatsApp is free, so forward it please, forward to as many as you can... Share this message with your loved ones... Note: Do not save this message, send it now to other groups you belong to. It is for your good and that of others, giving somebody relief is always rewarding.[30]

The first paragraph contains the name of the authority, Dr Okyere. A quick Google search shows that the message has appeared in other forums online, specifically on a WordPress blog. However, unlike the doctor in this WhatsApp message who is Nigerian, the doctor in the blogpost is Ghanaian. As such, it seems as though the doctor's nationality has been edited based on the audience's nationality. However, the composers of the message did not edit the name of the minister. Nigeria does not have a minister by the name mentioned in the message.

During the Covid-19 pandemic 'forwarded as received' health messages like this – unverified and largely untrue – advising readers on what to do to protect themselves against the virus were very common. Seven of the respondents admitted they sent 'forwarded as received' Covid-19 health messages because they believed they can be beneficial to other users. However, with these messages also flowed fake news:

Elderly people are trying to be informed so any information resembles solutions to the problem, then they take it serious even if they are unverified. They want to believe everything because they are looking for solutions ... We have seen information that is misinformation and that if you rely on them, you may suffer from other things.[31]

More than just sharing the forwarded messages, respondents like Olabisi Onanuga employed some of the advice. 'I read and at times, I made use of some of them. I practice them. I do forward messages to people, any health related messages, so that other people can learn from it. For instance, there was this one about boiling citrus fruits like lemon, lime and oranges and drinking the juice, which I did.'[32]

Recently, and reflective of current socio-political realities in Nigeria, there has been an increase in the dissemination of false information that aims to exacerbated pre-existing ethno-religious tensions. One message with serious ethno-political undertones was followed by a response from Olujimi, a member of the DTTC ERUWA '81 group.

> As a group comprising both Christians and Muslims and with different political leanings, we should refrain from circulating highly flammable publications like this one. We should be careful not to be used by politicians who are desperately planning for 2023. All this Fulani brouhaha is an agenda towards 2023 general elections.[33]

SK Olawumi, who is one of the administrators of the group, says that there are rules of engagement for members. Whenever a wrong message is sent, the defaulter is reprimanded according to the group's established rules which include an open rebuke on the platform. While this may work temporarily, sometimes they get carried away and repeat the action.[34]

Despite the community established rules on many WhatsApp groups, members still flout them. This shows that even though group administrators have tried to bring some form of decorum to the group, their methods do not always work. WhatsApp can do more to build more clearly into a group's architecture the information and rules for each group, in such a way that once users become members of specific groups, they immediately read the rules binding the group and agree to them. This would make it easier for group members to self-regulate themselves rather than to be punished by group administrators. When members fail to comply, there needs to be more support to educate users. The goal should be about education that supports behavioural change among elderly users, not punishment by blacklisting.

Learning as they go

When Olawoore started using WhatsApp, she only knew how to read messages that were sent to her. She could neither reply nor forward. However, with time and with her children's help, she learned not only how to reply to messages but also how to use other features – video call, voice call and even the status feature. Unlike many applications that have a 'walk-in' tutorial that takes you through their features and uses, WhatsApp is learned usually through repeated use or by observing more skilled users of the platform. For many of these seniors, these are usually their children, grandchildren on younger people in their communities. A positive consequence of this is that it allows some form of intergenerational interaction between the digital native and the digital illiterate. While this may be useful for some older users, many of them are still uneducated about responsible behaviour on the platform.

Whilst almost everyone interviewed for this study could make use of all the features – they could read, reply and forward messages; they could also make use of voice calls and voice messages even as they shared pictures – an ability to use all the features is different to their level of user awareness. Among Nigerian retirees, we can identify three broad levels of WhatsApp users; beginners, intermediates and advanced. These levels are not static, the spaces are fluid as the more 'WhatsApp-educated' respondents become, the more versatile in the use of WhatsApp features they are. However, dexterity and frequency of use is not enough to make many of them move between the final two levels. While some users like Olawoore started at the beginner level – characterized by infrequent usage and rare engagement beyond individuals within their immediate circle offline – more digital literacy on the platform can move them to the intermediate level. The intermediate user is one that is not only aware of the features but uses them, and has the capacity to abuse them. While the advanced user is aware of not only the features and their uses but also the potential for abuse and is wary of abusing the application. People in this category may even go one step ahead to try to correct other users of the application when abuse happens.

While WhatsApp allows retirees to continue offline conversations online, it also opens them to risks and falsehoods, especially when they are added to groups that they do not have offline connections with. Preventing or limiting the spread of fake news before it is sent is better than attempting to 'cure' after the content has been received. While WhatsApp presents a 'fluidity' of information flow by making it easy to connect and share information on the platform, more fact-checking measures have to be put in place to protect and support older users, coming to digital technology often for the first time in their lives. Rather than blaming older people for the spread of fake news, there should be more concerted efforts – in terms of platform transparency and education about different WhatsApp tools – that can empower older users to reduce the spread of falsehoods and better inform themselves.

Notes

1   See Yomi Kazeem. 2019. 'Forwarded as Received, WhatsApp is the Medium of Choice by Older Nigerians for Spreading Fake News'. *Quartz Africa*. 23 October. Available at https://qz.com/africa/1688521/ whatsapp-increases-the-spread-of-fake-news-among-older-nigerians/; Rianna Walcott. 2020. 'WhatsApp aunties and the spread of fake news'. *Wellcome Collection*. 7 July. Available at https://wellcomecollection. org/articles/Xv3T1xQAAADN3N3r; Adaobi Tricia Nwaubani. 2020. 'Letter from Africa: Why Nigerians are muting their mothers on WhatsApp'. *BBC*. 8 June. Available at https://www.bbc.com/news/world-africa-52927678

2 Nigeria Health Watch. 2020. 'WhatsApp for social good: How Nigerians used the platform to show care during the COVID-19 lockdown'. 30 June. Available at https://nigeriahealthwatch.com/whatsapp-for-social-good-how-nigerians-used-the-platform-to-show-care-during-the-covid-19-lockdown/

3 Simon Kemp. 2021. 'Digital 2021: Nigeria. Data Reportal'. 11 February. Available at https://datareportal.com/reports/digital-2021-nigeria

4 Monica Anderson and Andrew Perrin. 2017. 'Technology use among seniors'. Pew Research. 17 May. Available at https://www.pewresearch.org/internet/2017/05/17/technology-use-among-seniors/

5 Annie Dayani Ahada and Syamimi Md Ariff Lim. 'Convenience or nuisance? The "WhatsApp" Dilemma'. *Procedia Social and Behavioral Sciences* 155 (2014), pp. 189–96.

6 Yomi Kazeem. 2020. 'How a youth-led digital movement is driving Nigeria's largest protests in a decade'. *Quartz Africa*. 13 October. Available at https://qz.com/africa/1916319/how-nigerians-use-social-media-to-organize-endsars-protests/

7 Naima Hafiz Abubakar and Salihu Ibrahim Dasuki. 'Empowerment in their hands: Use of WhatsApp by women in Nigeria'. *Gender, Technology and Development* 22, 2 (2018), pp. 164–83.

8 Yomi Kazeem. 2020. 'Young Nigerian protesters are using social media to dispel misinformation from traditional media'. 14 October. Available at https://qz.com/africa/1917507/nigeria-endsars-protests-use-twitter-whatsapp-to-beat-fake-news/

9 Sharmila Nair. 2019. 'When the older generation become dependent on their smartphones'. *The Star*. 23 December. Available at https://www.thestar.com.my/tech/tech-news/2019/12/23/when-the-older-generation-become-dependent-on-their-smartphones

10 Mireia Fernández-Ardèvol, Kim Sawchuk and Line Grenier. 'Maintaining connections octo- and nonagenarians on digital "Use and Non-use"'. *Nordicom Review* 38 (2017), pp. 39–51.

11 Fernández-Ardèvol, Sawchuk and Grenier. 'Maintaining connections'.

12 Bong Way Kiata and Weiqin Chena. 'Mobile instant messaging for the elderly'. *Procedia Computer Science* 67 (2015), pp. 28–37.

13 Kiata and Chena. 'Mobile instant messaging'.

14 Monica Anderson and Andrew Perrin. 2017. 'Barriers to adoption and attitudes towards technology'. Pew Research. 17 May. Available at https://www.pewresearch.org/internet/2017/05/17/barriers-to-adoption-and-attitudes-towards-technology/

15 Nair. 'When the older generation become dependent'.

16 All respondents were informed that the interviews would form the basis for academic research and gave verbal consent to their names and insights to be used to the author.

17 Author's personal interview. February 2021.

18 Ibid.

19 Ibid.

20 Kenton O'Hara et al. 'Everyday dwelling with WhatsApp'. *Proceedings of the 17th ACM conference on Computer supported cooperative work & social computing* (2014), pp. 1131–42.

21 Mireia Fernández-Ardèvol and Andrea Rosales. 'Older people, smartphones and WhatsApp'. in Jane Vincent and Leslie Haddon (eds), *Smartphone cultures* (United Kingdom: Routledge, 2018), pp. 55–68.

22 Author's personal interview. February 2021.

23 Kazeem. 'Young Nigerian protesters'.

24 Author's personal interview. February 2021.

25 Ibid.

26 Ibid.

27 Ibid.

28 Ibid.

29 Information about the content shared by the group was obtained in two ways: one group member gave the author access to the group through her phone, whilst some members forwarded messages directly to the author that had been shared in the group.

30 DTTC Eruwa '81 WhatsApp Group. Accessed March 2021.

31 Author's personal interview. February 2021.

32 Ibid.

33 DTTC Eruwa WhatsApp Group. Accessed March 2021.

34 Author's personal interview. February 2021.

7

New media, social relationships and communication imperatives: A study of Christlove Fellowship Alumni WhatsApp groups

Feyisitan Ijimakinwa and Fortune Afatakpa

This chapter explores how alumni members of Christlove Fellowship, a faith-based student organization at Obafemi Awolowo University, Ile-Ife, Nigeria, used and continue to use WhatsApp to grow, promote social relationships and inclusion and deliver capacity development to its members. Drawing on the authors' membership of these WhatsApp groups that facilitated access to the varied discussions and interactions that go on in the groups, this chapter highlights the history, as well as structure of the alumni group, its day-to-day conversations, the networking and employment opportunities it offers and the training and other diverse activities it provides. In doing so it gives rich insight into the workings of this online community. In accordance with research ethics, and to respect the rights and privacy of members of the Christlove Fellowship Alumni WhatsApp groups, the true identities of members who were engaged or cited in proceedings, discussions and engagements for this study are not disclosed.

Feyisitan Ijimakinwa is a researcher at the Institute of African Studies, University of Ibadan, Nigeria. Fortune Afatakpa is a lecturer at Dominion University, Ibadan, Nigeria.

The Christlove Fellowship

Rhema Fellowship, a campus-based Christian group, was started in April 1985 by two female students – Kemi Santos and Toyin Jegede – of the then University of Ife (now Obafemi Awolowo University) in Ile Ife, southwest Nigeria. The student fellowship started with five students who gathered to pray together, and soon grew to fifteen. Rhema Fellowship soon changed its name to Christlove Fellowship (CLF) as its membership grew steadily. By the time CLF had been around for a year, the number of its regular members had grown to over fifty. The fellowship attracted young persons who identified as Christians but were distinct from the large mass of conservative Christian students on campus. This came as a rude shock to the established and influential conservative Christian community in the school.

These conservative Christian elements were easy to pick out, among the student populace in the Obafemi Awolowo University, as they were usually drably attired in dresses, gowns as well as long skirts that dropped below the knees. They shunned jewellery and other trendy looks, in keeping with the perception of evangelical Christianity in Nigeria in the late 1970s.[1] However, the new kid on the block, CLF was remarkably different as its members applied make-up, used jewellery and wore colourful outfits including trousers. Whilst the majority conservative Christian students represented the old, members of CLF symbolized a growing brand of American-influenced evangelical Christianity that was spreading amongst youths in Nigeria. Its unconventional style and practice did not only cause consternation in the school, but continued to record unbridled growth despite opposition from the Christian establishment on campus.[2]

The peculiarity of the situation with CLF was heightened by the fact that the fellowship was like an organic offshoot of the growing influence of American patterned churches and evangelical movements made popular by American televangelists. By the 1991–92 academic session, according to the records of the Directorate of Student Affairs of the university, CLF had grown to become the second largest student group in the school, with 547 members. In spite of the growth and expansion of CLF, it was not accepted into the Ife Joint Varsity Christian Union (IJVCU); the umbrella body of all student Christian fellowships at the university.[3] Invitations for participation in IJVCU programmes were not extended to CLF and members of CLF were constrained to become their own best friends as they were shunned in every aspect of Christian mutuality on campus.[4] This isolation forced the fellowship to become resourceful as it drew friends from similar groups in other schools across the country.

Student groups in many universities, especially the religious groups, show clear organizational abilities in managing their finances and in the deployment of diverse resources to execute projects and events.[5] The organizational structure that the fellowship established became a mainstay of the organization. Since 1988, the fellowship has held its annual convention tagged *Agape* celebration; a weeklong programme complete with word ministrations, musical shows, study sessions, as well as evangelistic activities. It used to draw huge attendances, especially from students from other institutions and is often complete with fanfare and pomp to the extent that the *Agape* celebration was regarded as the biggest assemblage of Christians in Obafemi Awolowo University in the 1990s.

The internal structure of CLF is determined spiritually, meaning that successors are divinely appointed and commissioned before the studentship of the outgoing set of leadership expires. The Board of Trustees is the highest body of the organizational structure whilst the Pastor (President) sits at the executive and spiritual head of the fellowship. There is a Vice President, as well as pastors of other outreach fellowships and heads of departments and units.

CLF has a very strong connection to its alumni. When members graduate from the university and, by extension, the fellowship, they are encouraged to keep in contact. This forges a link between the home fellowship at the university and alumni members. There is only one home fellowship at the university and eight alumni branches. Active branches include those situated in Lagos, Ibadan and Abuja in

Nigeria as well as internationally in the United Kingdom and North America. These groups meet regularly in all these locations, with the aim of continuously building membership and in an attempt to sustain relationships developed as students and members of the same fellowship. In addition, CLF has an official alumni association, a body that is formally registered with the Corporate Affairs Commission in Nigeria, with an estimated 2,500 members.

A peculiar feature of the CLF alumni association is its 'compound membership' system. This means that spouses of members of the alumni association are automatically recognized and accepted as members. This means that a spouse that gets into the association via this system is entitled to all privileges available to an original member. Some of these privileges include being able to contest for any elective position in the association, the opportunity to represent the association at any external forum, as well as the right to be addressed as a CLF alumnus or alumna. A spouse can aspire to any office in the body and is treated as an original member who graduated from the school fellowship. In the history of the alumni association, two members by marriage have served as presidents of the alumni association.

Furthermore, the alumni association also serves as resource base for new graduates from the school. Fresh graduates often leverage the connection and network of alumni members to negotiate their way through the maze of the search for internships or employment. Alumni help the new graduates to get a foothold in the labour market or give them a soft landing that makes it easy for them to get their first jobs and opportunities after graduation from school.

Mobilizing CLF alumni online

As the number of people that had passed through the home fellowship has grown, more members of the alumni association are spread across Nigeria and beyond. With this, the challenge of physical convergence for regular meetings of alumni members emerged. To address this, the alumni association decided to create a CLF Alumni Yahoo group in 2006. This was the alumni association's first attempt at a digital intervention. The platform served as the virtual notice board for all alumni activities, and as a veritable complement to the main physical meetings that were held once a month. The physical meetings were facing their own challenge as attendance was dwindling, with the socio-economic constraints and challenges that Nigeria faced in the late 1990s and early 2000s affecting the commitment of members to the activities of the alumni association.

To keep the association alive, the Yahoo group was created. However, the same hiccup that militated against the physical meetings of the alumni groups soon raised its head with the Yahoo group. The level of engagements soon dropped very low to the point that many people actually did not even know the platform existed. Members were not posting materials or resources, save for occasional motivational materials that were rarely read. The platform was failing to serve as the notice board to promote the activities of the alumni body. At the midpoint of the 2010s, a new set of graduate members of CLF fellowship, who desired a new lease of life between the home fellowship and the alumni association, sought to reactive its online presence on WhatsApp. Concerns about the lethargic state of the alumni association, including its regular physical convergence, especially in Lagos, had become a source of worry to this generation of members who were more familiar with the online environment.

On 15 October 2015, the first CLF Alumni WhatsApp group was created. It was designed to serve as the online platform for social interaction amongst members of the alumni association. The group was open to all association members including their spouses. At its inception, the WhatsApp group had only three administrators, but this has since grown to seven. There was no particular process to decide how the administrators of the group would be picked. However, the body of administrators reflects the diversity and captures, to a great extent, the different generations of Christlovers (as members of CLF are called) that have passed through the home fellowship.

The membership of the WhatsApp groups was subsequently built through invitations and information on the group extended to alumni members who then signed up to the group. The first CLF Alumni WhatsApp group was christened CLF Alumni Central, whilst there is also a CLF Alumni 2 popularly referred to as 'School 2'. The two groups, being the central alumni groups, house members who live in different parts of the world including, but not limited to, Nigeria, the United Kingdom, Asia and North America. The demographic composition of the members is diverse, and distributed along the lines of age, gender, profession, vocation and marital status.

There are no formal ground rules in the WhatsApp groups. But members are unified by the common denominator of being 'born again' Christians with strong socio-religious beliefs and values, and this guide engagements and interactions in the group. Members know indecent and unedifying images and posts are not welcome. But discussions about politics are. Members do not shy away from discussing politics – global and national – with everyone ready and permitted to take a position on matters that are discussed. To better understand the interactions that take place in these groups this chapter employs conversation analysis, drawing on insights gathered from the CLF Alumni WhatsApp groups that the authors are members of.

A day in CLF Alumni WhatsApp group

Members of the CLF alumni WhatsApp group often describe it as a twenty-four-hour active group. This speaks to the active membership as well as the different time zones to which members belong. This tallies with the position that virtual groups benefit from the 'continuity hoops' of members who can come into the chat rooms (pages) at different times, drop their views, comments, pictures and even set agendas which are picked up by other members at different times.[6]

But since most members are domiciled in Nigeria, the activities and presence for engagements are mostly led by members in Nigeria.

Early in the morning the first sets of devotionals by different members are posted in the group. These different devotionals are complete with Bible passages, central messages, prayers as well as memory verses, and they are regularly posted by certain members. The messages and prayers of the devotionals, set the tone for the early part of the day. As more members join the platform for the day, you also have daily confessions and affirmations that are often posted and used by members of the group. When these affirmations are posted, people use them and these are also complemented by music videos including hymns, of Nigerian or foreign music artists. This gives support to the position that learning as well as lifestyle patterns are learnt via social media.[7] Whilst no one sets the agenda for the day, usually the day begins on the note of inspiration, motivation, affirmation and confession. It soon devolves into banters, jokes, reactions and new topical issues that are not curated yet find their way in to the group.

In most cases, topical issues are brought to the group by members, either in response to developments that have been reported in the media or discussed in other groups to which members may belong. Rarely do members say outrightly that they want such and such issues to be discussed. Although WhatsApp is a private messenger application, group platforms, especially ones that have more than fifty individual members like the CLF alumni WhatsApp group, are mostly regarded as virtual 'micro' public sphere as people come in with their ideas, positions and observations that are informed by the offline experiences. Unlike a more formal meeting there is no set agenda. Members keep contributing their opinions and views, sometimes for days, and these are always attended by strong, lively and heavily referenced comments.[8]

For example, a member reposted a story from another WhatsApp group which she belonged about a woman who has three daughters with her husband. The husband had developed some renal problems and needed a kidney transplant. The wife, being a match, decided to donate a kidney to the husband. One day whilst getting ready to go ready to the hospital for the surgery, as she was sorting out some paperwork at home she came across the will to the husband's estate. To her surprise, the husband has three boys with another woman and had planned to leave 90 per cent of his estate to the three sons, leaving her and her three daughters with only 10 per cent of his estate. In desperation and disappointment, the woman had asked a counsellor what to do and if she should go ahead with the organ donation.

This post generated a robust argument on the platform. As a Christian group, one would have expected members to speak from the premise of forgiveness and love, strong principles of the Christian faith. However, some members argued that the cheating husband did not deserve any form of pity because he has been exposed for who he is – a liar and a cheat. An example of this is the comment of a member of the group, as written (typed) and captured below:

> Let me play the man's advocate small .... so his wife did not know about this other family... which means they have been severely deprived of his presence. The boys never enjoyed their father (don't ask me how he found time to birth them). He has been a good husband/father and provider to his real family .... they've enjoyed him well in his lifetime. The 90% is compensation for the loss which money cannot buy anyway in the lives of those 3 boys.[9]

The contributors attempt to make light of the matter was not welcome as many members, in clear terms, deplored the husband's unfaithfulness, wickedness and insensitivity. Most members that contributed to the conversation pointed out that the Christian tenets of faithfulness should not be mistaken for naivety. Several contributors said that the woman should not donate the kidney to the man. Some even indicted the lawyer who aided a legally married man to hide his unfaithfulness in marriage. A reaction from another member captured these sentiments:

> A fraudulent deceiver will come up with a more wicked scheme.... my challenge with Christians is how we label people. This guy has since stopped being a husband when he took the steps to go out there to impregnate another woman, three different times because he was looking for a particular gender. God knows why he gives what to whom. This is a deceiver not a husband. If asked to kill for his cause, he

may just do it because what's driving him is far too strong! I am sorry I feel no pity for him. Let's not advise the woman to remove her kidney for him at all. This kind of person has no plans for fatherhood… it's wickedness at its heights.[10]

Members of the CLF Alumni WhatsApp groups are professed Christians and therefore are more likely to be on the side of righteousness, justice, fairness and virtue. Therefore it is perhaps not surprising that many were outspoken and critical of the lies and infidelity of the sick husband. The exchange here reflects the position of members on socio-cultural issues like fidelity within the institution of marriage, which is a regular discourse, in both virtual and physical places in the Nigerian society. The interesting aspect of it is the candour of most members who were not unnecessarily tainted by the Christian tenet of forgiveness. From the foregoing, it can be suggested that the virtual nature of WhatsApp reduces the possible discomfort and other considerations by contributors to more sensitive topics of conversations. Virtual spaces support anonymity, to a certain extent, making it easier for people to express opinions with little or no consideration for socio-cultural underpinnings and colourations. Instead, people air their views and positions freely on taboo subjects; something that may be constrained by different factors in physical meetings and conversations.[11]

Accessing opportunities

CLF alumni WhatsApp group members draw heavily from the available resources of other members. One of the core areas where new and old members continue to benefit from is the regular posting of job opportunities by members. A couple of members who have information on genuine job openings and opportunities list these vacancies on the platform and members, as well as people known to them, are given top consideration for these jobs. It is important to note that though these job openings may not be a direct brief of the member that posts it, such members often know the agency or firm that is involved in the recruitment, and with references from a CLF Alumni member, the applicants' chances of getting these jobs are enhanced. WhatsApp, along with other social media platforms, is fast becoming a new business field where resources are accessed to the benefits of users of these new media.[12]

In some cases, human resources or recruitment agencies specifically ask that job listings, openings and opportunities should be only circulated in closed groups such as the CLF WhatsApp group. Thus, the group serves the purpose of helping people to access opportunities and facilitating employment for different people within the group or those associated with people within the group. In other instances, virtual trainings and workshops for job seekers or those who want to change jobs are facilitated for members on the platform. During the lockdown that was introduced to curb Covid-19 in Nigeria in April 2020, many jobs were lost. Like all Nigerians, this affected members of the group as well. To mitigate this and to help members to acquire necessary skills and trainings, not less than five virtual trainings were organized via WhatsApp as well as with Zoom. The free strategic trainings were offered in the areas of project management, wealth management, asset management, insurance and publishing. Access to such specialized trainings is tightly controlled and exclusive to members of the alumni association.

Closely connected with this, the group also organizes talk shops and seminars for members in strategic areas such as investment, wealth creation and personal finance. Experts in these key areas are invited to the group to share their insights and expertise. These initiatives draw attendance from a wide section of the group as members key into these programmes to get answers and insights on key areas of interest and concern. The advantage that comes with this is the fact that members can get premium advisory services and consultations for free. For example, during the lockdown that greeted the outbreak of the Covid-19 pandemic, the executives of the alumni association organized a series of virtual economic seminars that threw light on the implication of the pandemic on the Nigerian economy and its possible effects on global economy in the post pandemic period. The seminar series featured economists, financial consultants and fund managers as well as those involved in key economic policies of the government. They helped members get a proper understanding of issues of the economy, enabling them to make informed decisions on the same.

During the lockdown and the lull in economic activities, many members turned to these educational economic resources and enlightenment that came from the platform and they used these to help them in navigating the delicate waters of pandemic-induced economic challenges. A financial consultant who was part of the first economic seminar hosted on the group's platform had this to say:

> The CLF group made a remarkable impression on me because the group plugged in very strategically by organising the economic seminar for its members, especially against the backdrop of the unexpected challenges of the pandemic. Indeed, they have made available to their members, important resources that everyone, and I mean everyone will need to cope in a post-pandemic economy.[13]

It is certainly true that the financial lessons and insights provided members of the group with tools and knowledge to help them negotiate the difficult economic realities facing many Nigerians during Covid-19.

On another level, members of the group enjoy the benefit of getting top notch, professional counsel and opinions on issues of health, medication and health management. One of the most common posts on WhatsApp, especially in groups and community platforms, is the posting and re-posting of health issues including unsubstantiated claims and advice. The regularity of these posts and how easily they circulate makes it difficult to know their origin, or in most cases, the validity of the claims. Apart from the fact that members are 'fined'[14] for re-posting any message that had been posted earlier, they are also counselled to make sure that they verify sources and authenticity of posts before reposting on the group. Beyond this the group goes the extra mile by engaging various health professionals—medical doctors, pharmacists, health managers and advisors – within the group and getting their informed and professional responses to some of these claims and positions. This action is one of the main attractions of the group as it has helped in 'rightly' informing members concerning the issues of spurious and unproven claims and assertions as contained in many viral and recycled posts on social media.[15]

Beyond this, the group also enables members to get access to easy and free consultations with health professionals on the platform. In a country like Nigeria, where access to functional healthcare service can be considered a luxury, easy access to health professionals who are considered as 'family members' is a prize. Members get the opportunity to have a first consultation and professional referrals from members on the platform. One member, whose sister had a serious hearing problem, said that a specialist in the group was able to facilitate a major health check for her and played a strategic role in the lady's surgery. To him, the CLF Alumni WhatsApp group is the best thing that ever happened to any member of his family.

The group also serves as a go-to place for credible information on a range of subjects. Information on traffic situations is shared for the benefits of members to help them in decision-making especially as it concerns intra-city mobility within Lagos. Information on educational trainings, workshops and seminars are regularly advertised on the platform. The informal interaction and engagement of most group members make it easy for participants to access the benefits and opportunities that are available[16] and the anonymity of WhatsApp breaks the wall of separation making it 'a small space of endless interaction that defies many odds'.[17]

The group also lends itself to other social imperatives that benefit not only members but also the general public. Regular health talks and even discussions on policies are initiated, and members use the opportunity to insert their narratives and positions to social discourses in this area. The issue of corruption in the health sector is a regular discussion in the group, and they do not shy from calling out the government in this area, even when there are key government officials listed as members of the group. An example surrounds the perennial industrial disputes in the sector. Members have held different debates and discussions on the issue. They point out that, most times, the government fails to exert will power in confronting and tackling the various problems in the health sector. Most members in the group always point out that though as Christians they believe in divine health, as promised by God, it behoves the government to ensure that healthcare services are available to the wider populace, with little or no hindrance. With the privilege of inside information, at times, members can clearly see that the corruption in the system is the greatest crippling factor in the health sector, just like it does to many other sectors in the country, and criticize it.

But the group is not just critical of the government's healthcare inaction. The CLF alumni, using the mobilizing machinery of the WhatsApp group, have been consistent in the social cause of blood donations. The group is a recognized and trusted group by the Lagos University Teaching Hospital when it comes to blood donation drives and exercises. It mobilizes its members who voluntarily turn up to donate blood at the teaching hospital's blood bank, as their own way of supporting a critical component of healthcare provision in the community. The blood donation exercise is one of the most important 'non formal' annual events in the group's calendar of activities.

Talking politics

Different political events including campaigns, rallies, elections and post-election activities such as court cases always provide ample talking points and discourse for members on the platform. As part of build-up to general elections in 2019, a number of discussions were moderated on the group's WhatsApp platform to help members get rich insights into the complex workings of different political parties, political camps and politicians with a view to helping members in making informed choices in the elections. The group recognized the political influences of some politicians especially in Lagos state which was one of the key spots in the election. Members agreed that there is need for a political realignment and shift in the state. In the view of one member:

> Lagos cannot continue to be in the pocket of some individuals who are obviously feeding fact on the commonwealth of the people and who use their influence to muzzle the people. This has continued because of a prostrate opposition that has failed to take advantage of opportunities.[18]

Members of the group recognize that politics is essential and that is why, unlike many other groups, discussion of politics is allowed on the platform. What this has yielded to the group is that members freely air their opinions, critique government's policies and actions, as well turning the spotlight on politicians, political organizations and regulatory agencies and bodies. Whilst members are free to be part of any political party or hold any political beliefs or ideologies, the position of most members is informed by the need to critically engage the government and ensure that the citizenry get the best end of the stick when it comes to government-citizens relationships and engagements.

Party ideologies, electoral promises, electoral frauds, bad representation and other shortcomings of the political class do not escape the attention of members of the group. In the same vein, members do not fail to praise the government or its officials especially when they do creditably well. According to one member of the group:

> The CLF WhatsApp group is filled with politically savvy people who know what they want and what the government should be serving the people. Members there do not talk tongue in cheek, instead, they say it as it is. On more than one occasion, I have seen how my political mentor has been dragged for his stand on some important national issues. Everyone is always allowed to say his or her mind but one thing is that the views of the majority are objective and not personality driven in any way. If you perform, you get the praise and if you fail to perform you get the whip.[19]

Political discussions on the platforms are foregrounded in trust and openness and this encourages members to freely air their views without fear, let or hindrance even if such positions or information will be considered 'unsafe' in another setting. Trust is, therefore, of premium importance in the group.

Owing to the interconnectedness of members of the CLF Alumni WhatsApp group through the shared commonality of faith and having passed through the same Christian fellowship on campus, there exists a considerable level of trust amongst members. In this regard, it becomes easy for members to enjoy some privileges and favours that hitherto would have been difficult to access outside the group. Members extend assistance, resources and other forms of soft landing to one and other. It is commonplace to hear of members, new to some locations, being hosted or accommodated by members of CLF Alumni resident available in that location. In the WhatsApp groups, members who will be visiting new locations often ask if there are CLF alumni members in that location. Members are known to play host to those they did not even meet while in school without reservations, because of their shared faith and mutual trusts that comes with CLF alumni membership status.

Digital publics

Despite the limited number of people that can be added to a WhatsApp group, calls for the CLF group to migrate to a more accommodating application have not been successful. Even though Telegram, another private messenger application, accommodates a larger number of people and offers end-to-end encryption, CLF alumni members chose to have multiple WhatsApp groups (eight in total), primarily because of the robust and interactive features of the application as well as due to the application's wide popularity and acceptance. It is also widely used because it addresses the problems of location and time – two important factors that can hinder physical meetings.

What is clear is that the CLF alumni WhatsApp groups have continued to be a strategic platform for members; giving a soft landing for those fresh out of school, especially as they find their feet in the labour market, and delivering resources to many categories of members who leverage the networks, connections and relationships it offers to enrich their own lives. Despite the WhatsApp groups being essentially an assemblage of people who are joined by the commonality of the faith they share, having passed through the same Christian fellowship while in school, it has continued to evolve as a distinct, socially relevant group of members with an open and untainted worldview. The CLF Alumni WhatsApp group remains an easily accessible, rich and viable resource pool that costs little or nothing but delivers extensive socio-economic, cultural and political benefits to its members. However, the network – and similar structures which exist for many other institutions or education establishments – reinforces social stratification in Nigerian society, given that membership bestows certain exclusive privileges. While this is not a new development, it has taken a new shape as physical groupings are now replicated in the virtual space. Level playing fields are now tilted in favour of members of these groups, as they get exclusive information and opportunities that are not open to or accessible to other members of the society.

As this chapter has shown, the adoption and use of social media tools, especially private messenger applications such as WhatsApp, is blurring the division between physical and virtual spaces of socialization. This is made profound by the fact that many group activities have migrated to the virtual space or what we can call a digital public space,[20] away from the hitherto exclusive physical spaces of connection and convergence. This change has been strengthened by the restrictions on socialization and circulation occasioned by Covid-19. As the CLF Alumni example illustrates, the two modes of socialization and meeting – physical and virtual – are becoming increasingly interconnected and complementary, a convergence increasingly facilitated by WhatsApp.

Notes

1 A. K Aluko. 'The growth of student religious organization in Nigerian schools. 1965–2015'. *Journal of Beliefs and Values* 21, 2 (2019), pp. 13–29.
2 Aluko. 'Student religious organization in Nigeria'.
3 David Stark. 'In the name of the Father: Revisiting spiritual development in Nigeria school system'. *Journal of International Pedagogy* 13, 2 (2015), pp. 74–91.
4 Adeola. *Pentecostalism and the Generational Question in Nigerian Schools* (Lagos: Clarence Press Limited, 2015).
5 M. Obuze. 'Management and organisation and youth development in Nigeria'. *Nigerian Statesman.* 2019.
6 Roberto Dell'Anno, Thierry Rayna and Offiong Solomon. 'Impact of social media on economic growth – evidence from social media'. *Applied Economics Letters* 23, 9 (2016), pp. 633–6.
7 Terry Kind and Yolanda Evans. 'Social media for lifelong learning'. *International Review of Psychiatry* 27, 2 (2015), pp. 124–32
8 Monika Djerf-Pierre, Marina Ghersetti and Ulrkia Hedman. 'Appropriating social media'. *Digital Journalism* 4, 7 (2016), pp. 849–60.
9 Content accessed from CLF Alumni Central WhatsApp group, April 2021.
10 Ibid.
11 Marika Steenkamp and Nathalie Hyde-Clarke. 'The use of Facebook for political commentary in South Africa'. *Telematics and Informatics* 31 (2014), pp. 91–7.
12 See Olapade. *Social Media and the New Face of Socialisation in Nigeria* (Lagos: Clarendon Press, 2019).
13 Personal interview, Lagos, 2021.
14 It is important to note that though members are fined for infractions, that is just a symbolic representation as money is neither demanded from nor paid by erring members. The use of the word 'fine' by members is only symbolic of the attitude of the group to fake or unsubstantiated information.
15 Anne Rüggemeier. 'Shame and shamelessness in contexts of care and caregiving in Philip Roth's Patrimony (1991) and Sarah Leavitt's Tangles (2012)'. *European Journal of English Studies* 23, 3 (2019), pp. 263–80.

16 Yaron Ariel and Ruth Avidar. 'Information, interactivity, and social media, Atlantic'. *Journal of Communication* 23, 1 (2015), pp. 19–30.
17 Kate Azuka Omenugha et al. 'Celebrity culture, media and the Nigerian youth: negotiating cultural identities in a globalised world'. *Critical Arts* 30, 2 (2015), pp. 200–16.
18 Content accessed from CLF Alumni Central WhatsApp group, March 2021.
19 Content accessed from CLF Alumni 2 WhatsApp group, November 2020.
20 Duncan Omanga. 'WhatsApp as "digital publics": the Nakuru analysts and the evolution of participation in county governance in Kenya'. *Journal of Eastern African Studies* 13, 1 (2019), pp. 175–91.

8

Sharing the gospel: How Nigeria's Catholic community is building a WhatsApp congregation

Patrick Egwu

Technology and innovation are mixing with religion for moral and social change. Religious communities around the world are increasingly using smartphone-enabled social media technologies and platforms to engage and influence the opinions and values of their congregation in the word of the gospel. These online tools can break barriers by meeting people in the comfort of their homes. As of January 2020, there were 169.2 million mobile phone connections and 85.49 million internet users in Nigeria; a 42 per cent penetration rate. Twenty-seven million of those were active social media users, with estimates suggesting that by 2023 the number will have risen to 36.8 million.[1]

The Catholic community in Nigeria is embracing the digital disruption of social media to create an online congregation. Priests and ministers now have what they call an 'online pulpit'. Masses and church programmes are streamed online with thousands of church goers joining in. Gospel messages are circulated and shared through extensive WhatsApp groups.

This has only increased amid the Covid-19 pandemic, during which there have been bans or limits on physical gatherings and communion. The Catholic community in Nigeria has found hope in Twitter, Facebook, WhatsApp, Instagram and video sharing communities like YouTube to reach their congregation who need succour and relief from

Patrick Egwu is a journalist and an Open Society Foundations fellow on Investigative Reporting at the University of Witwatersrand.

the impact of the global health crisis. In addition, congregations for sisters of the Catholic church across Nigeria are staying connected and sustaining their ministries and spiritual lives using WhatsApp. The application creates a platform for the sisters to grow their religious lives, share the gospel with local communities where they live, and raise awareness and information about the pandemic. WhatsApp is breaking boundaries and facilitating this everyday communication and conversations among, and between, religious communities.

This partially explains why the government's plans to regulate social media in the country have been strongly opposed by the Catholic community in Nigeria.[2] In November 2019, lawmakers at Nigeria's National Assembly introduced two bills which they said would help fight hate speech and fake news on the internet.[3] The bills, if passed into law, would penalize offenders with payment of fines, prison time or the death penalty. Bishops and priests have argued the move would stifle not only the freedom of expression guaranteed by the constitution but also their ability to use the media for the spread of the gospel which has seen them reach out to their congregation despite physical restrictions and other barriers. Civil society activists agree. Lanre Arogundade, the executive director of the International Press Council, a Nigerian-based media non-profit media which advocates for press freedom, argues the proposed laws seek to instil fear on the citizens and make the media publish only information or materials that are pro-government. 'The laws seek to criminalize free speech ... they are anti-press freedom despite their argument that they want to curtail hate speech. There are other existing laws [like cybercrime law] that take care of issues of internet and social media hateful information.'[4]

For this chapter, I conducted dozens of interviews with priests, sisters, directors of Catholic institutes and non-profits, and drew on my own personal experiences, to learn more about how the church utilizes WhatsApp to reach a digital congregation. In addition, a desk review of Catholic documents and papers produced by the Vatican Council supported a better understanding of the place of the church and social media as a means of propagating the gospel. In the analysis of these, this chapter aims to further broaden the scope of previous research on religious interfaces with social media and digital technologies, such as WhatsApp, for sharing the gospel,[5] while providing an in-depth analysis and contexts into the issue of usage, challenges and way forward for best practices and better engagement with congregation in sharing the gospel in Nigeria.

Spreading the gospel on social media

For more than a decade, spreading the gospel through social media has become one of the dominant features of Catholic communities in Nigeria in the face of growing innovation and technological disruptions. The church and its pastors are taking the gospel message to where their congregations increasingly are – social media platforms and private messenger applications. Church goers in the Catholic communities in Nigeria are active internet users and often use the platforms or applications for interactions and exchanging ideas and thoughts. Catholics are found in virtually every community across Nigeria, aligned to a local parish with a presiding priest under the authority of a diocese. In 2017, there were 28.8 million in Nigeria, according to the Vatican's *Statistical Yearbook of the Church*.[6]

But Catholic communities in Nigeria were latecomers to the use of social media for the spread of the gospel. In the early 2000s, the use of technology was not popular among the Catholic church in Nigeria. At that time, they relied more on their large population and the affinity of members to the faith. Parishes and priests did not see or fully realize the power of platforms like WhatsApp to spread the gospel and engage their congregation. At that time, it was Pentecostal denominations who were more deeply engaged in the use of this technology to reach out to their congregation online.

However, the use of different means of communication for evangelism has a long history in the Catholic church. In December

1963, the Second Vatican Council under Pope Paul VI published *Inter Mirifica*[7] – which translates to 'among the wonderful' – and specifically refers to the use of movies, radio and television as means of social communication and propagating the gospel. Although there was no social media at that time, the contents of the Vatican document hint at future technological innovations and advancement in the present means of communications and the impact it would have on the church's evangelization. The emphasis of the document, and the essential concern of the Council, were to educate all Catholics on the importance of using communication tools responsibly, for the common good, and to enhance the apostolic ministry of the Church. The first chapter of the document reads:

> It is, therefore, an inherent right of the Church to have at its disposal and to employ any of these media insofar as they are necessary or useful for the instruction of Christians and all its efforts for the welfare of souls. It is the duty of Pastors to instruct and guide the faithful so that they, with the help of these same media, may further the salvation and perfection of themselves and of the entire human family. In addition, the laity especially must strive to instil a human and Christian spirit into these media, so that they may fully measure up to the great expectations of mankind and to God's design.[8]

'The document said among all the wonderful things humans have created, they have created and developed the means of social communication which has the power of entrenching good values but also has the power to destroy things,'[9] argues Fr. Jude-Mary Owoh, the director of media for the Dominicans[10] in Nigeria and Ghana. Fr. Owoh is an expert in the use of social media for evangelization in the Catholic Church in Nigeria. He sees communication as a critical part of its work.

> When Pope John Paul II started his pontificate as Pope, he said that the church must begin anew, to begin an era of new evangelisation. With that, he already set into motion the need to use every possible means of communication which was radio, television and newspapers to spread the word of God… and now that social media has come

about, it is also a means. You will be shocked how many Catholic social media accounts exist today in Nigeria. More people are beginning to understand and adapt it as a means of enriching their faith.[11]

While announcing the fiftieth World Communication in January 2016, Pope Francis affirmed social media as a gift from God saying 'emails, text messages, social networks and chats' can be 'fully human forms of communication'.[12] Sharing the gospel through social media, touching lives and engaging and influencing the wider Catholic communities in Nigeria are now an integral part of hundreds of tech-savvy priests and local parishes in the country. There is undoubtedly growing popularity for online congregations which have been made possible by social media.

The internet ministry

When Fr. Owoh got his first mobile phone in 2008, he would share text messages with friends which were mostly brief summaries of the Bible readings at church. But in 2009 he discovered WhatsApp and Facebook, created an account and started posting those spiritual reflections he used to send to friends through text messages on the platforms.

> I have always been a person who is in tune with using whatever I can find around me to disseminate information ... I have always been a fan of sharing my faith to people, so when I first learned of that media of communications [social media], I decided to use them creatively, and I also realised that some of my friends had also created Facebook accounts.[13]

A year after creating his WhatsApp and Facebook accounts, Fr. Owoh joined Twitter and realized that he could link both accounts in a way that whatever he posts on Facebook also appears on Twitter. In 2012 when he discovered Instagram, he created an account and joined as a way of having different means of sharing the gospel. Cross-posting across platforms in Nigeria is very common. But Fr. Owoh specifically uses WhatsApp to disseminate gospel messages, memory verses, short reflections and spiritual motivations to hundreds of friends and followers on his contact list and other closed-groups he belongs to.

When the province of St Joseph the Worker of the Dominicans in Nigeria and Ghana decided to establish a ministry for the use of social media, called the Ministry of Internet and Media in 2017, Fr. Owoh was appointed the deputy promoter because of his expertise and competency. 'I was charged with the creation of content for the purpose of reaching people … I realised that the greater demographic of people who used the internet are young people between the ages of 13–35, so I started to create contents tailored towards their needs.'[14]

Daily reflections and weekly videos and programmes are some of the activities of the ministry including one of their biggest programmes – *Catholic Faith Forum*, a 30-minute talk show streamed live on YouTube that addresses issues of faith, morals and popular culture. After the show, Fr. Owoh shares short clips on his WhatsApp status and posts the link to the full video where those on his contact list can go and watch. Since 2017, the YouTube programme of ministry has accumulated more than 3,000 subscribers, with many more content recipients across social media platforms and private messenger applications where the clips and links are shared.

Social media has shown priests and the church that you cannot just wait for people to gather on a Sunday for them to hear the word of God. That you need to find a way of getting the message across to people where they are. Social media has become that place: a place where people come to meet and interact for the purpose of relationship and exchange of ideas and in this marketplace of communication and interaction, the gospel is also looking to find relevance. Fr. Ugochukwu Ugwoke, a priest of the Institute of Schoenstatt Fathers in Nigeria's southwest region, runs what he calls an 'online pulpit' where he shares the gospel and engages mostly young Catholics across social media platforms and on WhatsApp.

> Where do they usually congregate when they are not in Church? It is online … the average Nigerian owns a smartphone and is connected

to the internet especially platforms like WhatsApp. They are there gaining and disseminating information in real time. So, they need the word of God administered to them as a way of breaking through the chaos and challenges of life they find themselves in.[15]

Fr. Ugwoke says he broadcasts and shares gospel reflections on WhatsApp groups he belongs to. Members of the group comment and share the messages with their friends or individual groups they belong to. This way, the gospel messages reach a wide audience and online congregation. Fr Ugokwe agrees that cyberspace has become a new mission field.

> Today, they have become another pulpit where I preach the word of God. One of the benefits of Twitter for example is that there is no limit or boundary as to who gets your message. Your audience is not limited. I remember Cardinal Zen of Hong Kong commenting on one of my tweets. Without social media, our paths would possibly never have crossed. Times have changed and the Church must be fully involved all over the world, where God acts and where the people are. Now, our age and people are thoroughly mediated and so, the media continuously shape their values and choices... I use my social media handles to preach the word of God, teach the faith and to refute errors against my faith. Our people need to know the right thing concerning the faith. If as ministers, we are not online to teach them the right thing, they will learn the wrong thing from the world or from other people posing as men and women of God.[16]

The communications department of the Catholic diocese of Awka in southeast Nigeria runs their outreach programmes through social media. A mobile application that is linked to their WhatsApp groups and Facebook accounts has also been developed. It contains information about the diocese including the number of parishes and priests, details of their creation and publications and events taking place at the diocese.

> We want people to be able to hold their smartphone and connect to their parishes. When people are in touch with the leaders of their church and with events and programmes taking place, then evangelisation is

going on … Now people can dialogue, interact, ask questions, evaluate, air their opinion and make contributions because you have given them a platform and with this, they don't need to book appointments with the bishop or priests.[17]

At the diocese, priests use WhatsApp for pastoral engagements and a dedicated WhatsApp group is used to disseminate information about diocese or other religious events. Priests engage with the information and schedule their activities around it, so they no longer have to drive away from their parishes to attend council meetings or receive information from the church secretariat. These also currently happen through WhatsApp. The platform also serves as a place where priests share ideas and new initiatives or solutions to problems that may arise during evangelization.

This innovation has come to stay and the church is employing that as much as possible to aid in the spread of the gospel ….a number of priests and parishes also have large social media followings because of their personality, teachings and homilies where they encounter and spread the gospel to people.[18]

Individual Catholics are also utilizing the opportunities provided by their individual platforms to spread the gospel to their followers and peers. Every Sunday, Henry Ihuoma, a young Catholic, uses his Facebook page of about 5,000 followers to share and explain the Bible readings of the day. Like Ihuoma, Cornelius Ndubuisi creates short messages and spiritual reflections and shares across WhatsApp groups he is a part of. These two individual examples are certainly not isolated. Thousands more Catholics in the country are using social media to spread the gospel to their peers and the wider Christian community.

Congregating during Covid-19

The global health crisis caused by the Covid-19 pandemic presented pressing challenges for the Catholic Church. In the early days of the outbreak, churches around the world closed their doors to parishioners, the first time church doors and physical communion around the world was restricted in almost a century.

But on social media, Catholics communities found refuge. Holy Masses were live-streamed on Facebook, Twitter and YouTube, and short clips shared on WhatsApp groups run by the local parishes. During Nigeria's nationwide lockdown in March 2020, social media enabled parishioners to worship together in a virtual space without even leaving the comfort of their homes. Priests and parishes with large online followings used Facebook and WhatsApp to organize church events and programmes that were previously done in a physical setting. If the church event was taking place on Facebook for instance, the parish coordinator of the WhatsApp group would communicate the time and day to the members so they could join and participate, illustrating the importance of cross-platform information sharing in the Nigerian context.

At the archdiocese of Lagos, a media programme runs online for parishioners in the region. The Archbishop of Lagos, Alfred Adewale Martins, gives a daily reflection both in audio and video formats to help the faithful connect with God wherever they may be. The videos, reduced in size, are then shared on WhatsApp in the church groups to which hundreds of members of the congregations belong.

Priests and ministers are also using their individual Facebook and WhatsApp platforms to share the gospel. Even as many digital disruptions are taking place around the world, ministers are still finding ways of reaching their flock to disseminate the message of hope and salvation through online technologies. Fr Ugokwe believes that:

> The Covid-19 pandemic has taught us the importance of the use of the tools of social media for evangelisation. When the church buildings were locked, it became the avenue through which most priests reached out to their flock, pastorally … what I noticed therefore is an increased awareness of the benefits of social media for evangelisation. Today, many dioceses, bishops, priests and even lay faithful have a strong presence on social media where they share the word with the world.[19]

Even when Nigeria announced the lifting of restrictions on places of worship in June 2020, attendance was capped at 50 per cent of the church's normal population. Furthermore, churches faced increasing risk of widespread cases of the virus as most places of worship deal with influx of members and little resources or preparedness to provide safety measures. With many members unsure about return to the physical church, a handful came to rely on a mobile application developed by Nnamdi Udeh, a young Catholic tech entrepreneur and his team in 2018, called OSanctus. The application supports virtual worshipping and helps in reducing overcrowding in the church as members can make reservations for seats some days before coming to church from the comfort of their homes. It was specifically designed to help digitize the whole church process in the country.[20]

Amid the pandemic, its functions have been redirected to meet the needs of the parishioners and churches such as streaming masses online, making payments and donations, or booking a virtual appointment with a local priest without physical contact. The application, which has been downloaded more than 500 times, runs in six parishes in Lagos, southwest Nigeria. 'It came in handy during the pandemic,' said Fr Paul Akin-Otiko who is a pastor at a Catholic-run chaplaincy where the application is used. 'We stream masses and post announcements, so our members can pick up. At the introduction, people were skeptical about the app but as they got on it, they started seeing the usefulness and started adjusting.'[21]

Building WhatsApp sisterhoods

In addition to furthering engagement with parishioners, WhatsApp is also helping to build connections between church officials and parish functions. During the pandemic, WhatsApp was used by the Daughters of Divine Love (DDL) congregation located in Enugu, southeast Nigeria. A closed WhatsApp forum created by the parish's sisters for easy communication allowed them to share the latest information about the pandemic as a way of raising awareness and to help them make informed decisions. The DDL congregation also runs a small charity home comprising more than fifty homeless and abandoned street children. With the information received from the WhatsApp forum about the virus and how it spreads, they could better educate the children in the home on safety precautions. As part of their ministry of reaching out and engaging with the communities where they live, the DDL congregation discusses approaches on how best to engage communities in the group. In most cases, the sisters could take decisions on how to distribute relief supplies to the members of the community and discussed how best to do this and how to make purchases through the WhatsApp group.

The DDL sisters are not the only example. The Sisters of Notre Dame de Namur (SND), also headquartered in the southeastern state of Enugu, also use WhatsApp groups for sharing information and spreading the gospel. During the pandemic, a WhatsApp group created by the sisters some years ago for easy communication about their ministry was turned into a go-to resource centre for news, data and tips on how to respond to the outbreak in the various ministries and communities they work in. Illustrating how information received and shared on the application has real-world applications and uses. The WhatsApp forum also served as means of communicating and sharing information with their colleagues on educating and raising awareness to local communities about human trafficking and social justice which are at the heart of their ministries outreach work.

Nigeria has one of the highest rates of human trafficking in Africa. The International Organization for Migration estimates that of the 181,000 migrants who travelled by sea from Libya to Italy in 2016, more than 37,000 were Nigerian, with Nigerian women and unaccompanied children accounting for 11,009 and 3,040 travellers, respectively.[22] About 80 per cent of the women returned had experienced sexual exploitation. Sr. Eucharia Madueke, of the SND congregation, is also the coordinator of African Women Project at the Africa Faith and Justice Network (AFJN) – a Washington-based Catholic advocacy non-profit. She has been integral to the work of the non-profit in using social media and other technologies to fight human trafficking, promote their work and educate local communities across Nigeria on the dangers of human trafficking. Since it was established in 1983, AFJN has been working with Nigeria's Catholic community and sisters from twenty-eight congregations to promote peace, advocate for human rights and organize online workshops. And since January 2021, Madueke's SND congregation and AFJN have been using WhatsApp groups and online meetings to plan anti-trafficking events. Several online meetings have been held on the issue with efforts made to raise awareness through street advocacy and campaigns and by meeting political actors, local lawmakers, and the police to urge them to take action on human trafficking.

In Lagos, Sr. Gloria Ozuluoke of the Religious Sisters of Charity uses social media to raise awareness on human trafficking and share the works of their congregation in local communities across the country. For instance, through a group chat on WhatsApp, the sisters share anti-trafficking information among themselves which helps them in raising awareness in communities where they work. They also coordinate their activities through WhatsApp and take action against human trafficking by working and sharing information with the local government, security agencies and other non-profits involved in fighting traffickers.

They also use it to mobilize and strategize against the different schemes used by the traffickers to lure unsuspecting victims from the rural areas. Traffickers often go to rural communities to make false promises and convince parents to give away their children so they can be taken to the city for non-existent job opportunities or football or modelling careers. But the sisters counter these moves by visiting these communities and educating the parents of the children through the information and plans they gather through WhatsApp. According to Sr. Ozuluoke,

> these WhatsApp groups help us to organise programmes and identify with people in local communities such as community leaders, schools and parishes so they can receive timely information of any moves for human trafficking.[23]

Recently, during the 'Prayer Marathon' – a seven-hour online event organized by the International Committee of the World Day and coordinated by Talitha Kum – the network of consecrated life against trafficking in persons of the International Union of Superiors General, Sr. Ozuluoke and other congregations in the country, led by the Committee for the Support of the Dignity of Woman – an anti-trafficking non-profit and home for victims established in 1999 – participated and featured in a 15-minute video-streamed live on YouTube that was also shared across WhatsApp. The global impact created by their work, which is coordinated and planned on the private messenger application, shows how the sisters are not prevented by geographical boundaries in sharing their work with the global community. In fact, the work of the sisters shows how online discussions and conversations are not simply confined to the online space, but taken offline, amplified and even implemented.

Overcoming challenges

For the Catholic church, the potential negative impact of social media for the purpose of evangelism or sharing of the gospel has always been a source of concern. For example, the 1963 decree on the media of social communication maintained:

> For the proper use of these media, it is most necessary that all who employ them be acquainted with the norms of morality and conscientiously put them into practice in this area. They must look, then, to the nature of what is communicated, given the special character of each of these media. At the same time, they must take into consideration the entire situation or circumstances, namely, the persons, place, time and other conditions under which communication takes place and which can affect or totally change its propriety. Among the circumstances to be considered is the precise manner in which a given medium achieves its effect. For its influence can be so great that men, especially if they are unprepared, can scarcely become aware of it, govern its impact, or, if necessary, reject it.[24]

A key challenge facing priests and ministers in their use of WhatsApp and other social media platforms is that they are competing against a huge amount of other content of varying levels of accuracy. Unlike in a physical church where they have the attention of the individual or congregation, online it is important that the contents of the message are designed in such a way it grabs the attention of the audience. There are also many online users who are not interested in hearing what the church has to say and may respond accordingly:

> Unlike mainstream media, social media has no external editor, almost no restriction. You think, you share or sometimes you share before even thinking. So sometimes, you see people who interact with your post in a very insolent and shocking manner, and you have to restrain yourself from stooping that low. You have some agnostics who make jest of your cherished beliefs and even some non-Christians.[25]

Regardless of the quality of the contents they create, and the resources invested in producing them, Fr. Owoh believes a major challenge stems from the fact that a lot of people are not looking out for religious contents including those who create them. Comedy skits, music videos and other celebrity contents that have more acceptability among social media users and have more tendency to be shared and promoted than gospel messages from the Christian perspective in his view.

> I work with a team and sometimes they find it difficult sharing the content they have created largely because their friends are not enthused with religious contents... it is an ongoing struggle, but we keep pushing and motivating each other to reach out with the contents we produce.[26]

Fr. Ugwoke agrees with Owoh, adding that the language of the gospel is opposed to most of the contents on social media platforms and as a result, most people see social media handles that preach the gospel and post religious contents in a less positive light:

> Most Catholics, especially the youth, are shy to profess their faith publicly. Many do not want to be identified as Catholics on social media....I have spoken to a few and even written an article to encourage such people not to shy away from using whatever means at

their disposal for evangelism. Even so, you do not underrate the power of one single post. One post is able to convert a straying soul or to bring relief to one who is suffering.[27]

Furthermore, knowing how to use and navigate WhatsApp is a challenge for some users. This is true of both members of the congregations and some priests and ministers who are not tech-savvy or digitally literate. There is also the challenge of internet accessibility and the cost of data and electronic gadgets such as smartphones or portable devices, especially for people in the rural areas. The cheapest smartphone which can run apps like WhatsApp can sell for US$100. This in a country battling to implement a new monthly minimum wage of ₦30,000 (about US$80). Lack of network access is also a huge challenge for congregations in rural communities who might want to access gospel messages through WhatsApp for example, but cannot. Yet even here WhatsApp is having an indirect impact as the sisterhood groups discussed in this chapter have illustrated, meaning that discussions on WhatsApp are penetrating into areas with little, or no, internet connectivity.

The use of WhatsApp as a platform for evangelism among the Catholic community in Nigeria is growing. New standards and ways of worship are being set and priests are now creating online religious communities, in addition to their offline ones, albeit with some overlap, that engage with the gospel of whether they attend church on Sunday or not. Many parishes in Nigeria without an online presence or WhatsApp forums for engaging their congregation and disseminating information about their activities with immediate feedback options, are starting to feel left behind. It is increasingly a matter of 'get in' or 'get shut out' from the world of rapid diffusion.

Notes

1   Simon Kemp. 2021. 'Digital 2021: Nigeria. *Data Reportal*. 11 February. Available at https://datareportal.com/reports/digital-2021-nigeria

2   Patrick Egwu. 2020. 'Nigerian Catholics protest bills aiming to regulate social media'. *National Catholic Reporter*. 24 February. Available at

https://www.ncronline.org/news/media/nigerian-catholics-protest-bills-aiming-regulate-social-media

3   Timileyin Omilana. 2019. 'Nigerians raise alarm over controversial Social Media Bill'. *Al Jazeera*. 18 December. Available at https://www.aljazeera.com/news/2019/12/18/nigerians-raise-alarm-over-controversial-social-media-bill

4   Personal interview with Lanre Arogundade, executive director, International Press Council, 15 December 2021.

5   See Fagunwa Omololu Ebenezer. 'Church growth and information communication technology: A case study of Nigeria and United Kingdom. 2015.' Thesis submitted for Masters of Theology. September: Kemi Ogunsola and Dare Adisa Raji. 'Qualitative study of the use of social media by church personnel for religious activities in Ibadan, Nigeria'. *African Journal for the Psychological Studies of Social Issues.* November 2019: Gerald Musa. 'Catholic church in Nigeria: The challenges of the use of social media.' *Nigeria Catholic Priests Discourse Forum.* June (2018).

6   Statistical Yearbook of the Catholic Church. 'Population of Catholics in Nigeria'. *Catholics and Culture.* 2017.

7   Pope Paul IV. 1963. 'Inter Mirifica: Decree on the media of social communications'. *The Vatican.* 4 December. Available at https://www.vatican.va/archive/hist_councils/ii_vatican_council/documents/vat-ii_decree_19631204_inter-mirifica_en.html

8   Pope IV. *Inter Mirifica.*

9   Personal interview with Fr Jude-Mary Owoh, director of media for the Dominicans in Nigeria and Ghana, 25 February 2021.

10 The Dominicans, which he belongs to, are a 70-year-old male religious group within the church that is dedicated to preaching with various means for the salvation of souls.

11 Interview with Fr Owoh.

12 Pope Francis. 2016. 'Communication and mercy: A fruitful encounter'. *The Vatican.* 24 January.

13 Interview with Fr Owoh.

14 Interview with Fr Owoh.

15 Interview with Fr Ugochukwu Ugwoke of the Institute of Schoenstatt Fathers, Ibadan Nigeria's southwest region. 26 February 2021.

16 Interview with Fr Ugwoke.

17 Interview with Fr Martin Anusi, the communications director, Awka Catholic diocese. 23 February 2021.

18 Interview with Fr Anusi.

19 Interview with Fr Ugwoke.

20 NPR staff. 2020. 'How 6 problem-solvers tackled pandemic challenges in their neighborhoods'. *Goats and Soda*. 12 July. Available at https://www.npr.org/sections/goatsandsoda/2020/07/12/888919603/how-6-problem-solvers-tackled-pandemic-challenges-in-their-neighborhoods

21 Interview with Fr Paul Akin-Otiko, chaplain, St Thomas Moore Catholic Chaplaincy, University of Lagos. 10 December 2020.

22 International Organization for Migration. 'Human Trafficking Along the Central Mediterranean Route'. 2017.

23 Sr. Gloria Ozuluoke in Patrick Egwu. 2021. 'Sisters fight Nigeria trafficking with networking, advocacy and collaboration'. *Global Sisters Report*. 20 May. Available at https://www.globalsistersreport.org/news/ministry/news/sisters-fight-nigeria-trafficking-networking-advocacy-and-collaboration

24 Pope IV. *Inter Mirifica*.

25 Interview with Fr Evaristus Bassey, former director of CARITAS Nigeria. 26 February 2021.

26 Interview with Fr Owoh.

27 Interview with Fr Ugwoke.

9

Amplifying female voices in northern Nigerian politics: The role of WhatsApp

Na'ima Hafiz Abubakar

Mobile penetration rates across Africa are growing exponentially; by the end of 2018, there were 456 million unique mobile subscribers on the continent, an increase of twenty million over the previous year.[1] Information and Communication Technology (ICT) is helping to transform people's realities by providing opportunities for the enhancement of socio-economic well-being. This is mainly driven by a belief that greater access to mobile phones and the internet has the potential to create economic growth and inclusive development on the African continent particularly for marginalized groups, such as women.

But studies[2] investigating the link between ICTs and the socio-economic well-being of women show evidence that women benefit less from the information society than men. Certain contextual factors such as restrictive cultural norms and practices and patriarchy and gendered roles place women at a disadvantage and among vulnerable groups that are excluded from society. This offline exclusion is reflected online. However, widespread social media use and its introduction into the domain of politics have brought about significant changes in the way citizens engage with politics. This study focuses on expanding that understanding to better explain the impact of WhatsApp use on female political participation in Nigeria. Although Facebook and YouTube are also popular mediums for communication, WhatsApp is the most ubiquitously used application in northern Nigeria, and across the African continent as a whole.[3]

Na'ima Abubakar is a lecturer at the Department of Information Technology, Bayero University, Kano.

The popularity of WhatsApp amongst Nigerian internet users can be attributed to factors such as its ease of use, low data consumption and perceptions of strong privacy features. Users prefer the closed network nature of WhatsApp which ensures that only contacts on a user's mobile phone have access to users' profile. This is further augmented by the feature that allows a user to select which of his or her contacts can view their status and status updates. WhatsApp also consumes less data in comparison to other applications. In Nigeria, all major mobile operators offer stand-alone data packages for rates as low as ₦200 (US$0.50) making it relatively affordable for many Nigerians. Additionally, WhatsApp's ease of use – the voice note feature that allows users to record and listen to messages – is another determinate of its widespread adoption.

The role of ICTs in Nigeria's elections has grown increasingly prominent since 2015 when the incumbent president Goodluck Jonathan lost to the main opposition leader Muhammadu Buhari. Smart card readers, used for voter authentication and verification, were first introduced in this election. Furthermore, results collated was updated and broadcasted live across various channels including social media platforms such as Facebook and Twitter, and on WhatsApp. Both leading political parties – the now opposition People's Democratic Party (PDP) and the ruling All Progressives Congress (APC) – and other smaller political parties have increasingly recognized the vital role that social media plays in the dissemination of information and the mobilization of voters. Almost all aspirants and candidates seeking, or holding elective office, at both federal and state levels now appoint special aides on 'new media'.

This chapter focuses on how women in northern Nigeria are using WhatsApp to participate in social and political life. It aims to better understand how WhatsApp is providing a virtual space for these women to express themselves in these settings. To provide an in-depth understanding of how this unfolds in practice for who and why, it draws on a case study of women's use of WhatsApp in the northern Nigerian city of Kano and qualitative research methods such as semi-structured interviews, focus groups and participant observation for data collection and analysis. The research is part of an ongoing study investigating the link between ICTs and female empowerment in Nigeria. The first round of data collection took place in December 2016, with subsequent rounds taking place in 2017, 2018 and 2019. Kano state, the second most populous state in Nigeria, accounted for 6.8 million out of the 122.6 million internet subscribers in 2019 according to the Nigerian Bureau of Statistics. A majority of these active mobile subscribers use WhatsApp. The platform has eaten into the traditional short message service (SMS) and voice call platforms provided by the major mobile operators such as Glo, MTN and 9mobile.[4]

Seven focus groups and twenty-four interviews were held with female WhatsApp users in Kano, selected from different parts of the city. Although all female, there were demographic differences in relation to age, marital status, education and income. This allows for comparisons between the women themselves and provides us with a better understanding of the way they interpret the effect WhatsApp use had on their lives. The interviews included women who worked as government officials in the Kano State Ministry of Women Affairs and Social Development; those who lectured at Bayero University, Kano; women leaders from the two leading political parties in Nigeria; female Islamic scholars; administrators of a multitude of WhatsApp groups; local business women; and female community leaders. Women deal with a multitude of roles and are constantly negotiating their different roles. The nature of this sample demonstrates the complex web of people involved in achieving improvement in women's lives.

Findings illustrate how women in northern Nigeria are using WhatsApp to receive and keep up-to-date with information about government and politics. Through membership of multiple WhatsApp groups, women access information and make vital decisions such on who to vote for in upcoming elections, interact with political representatives and contribute more to political discussions in their communities. These women are using WhatsApp in ways that enables them to participate in the sociopolitical life of society by conforming and in some ways reforming cultural offline practices that previously restricted them from doing so. But online and offline worlds continue to interact with respondents noting that when judging the authenticity of information they tend to make decisions based on their personal relationship with the sender.

Group life

The WhatsApp groups studied replicate real-life social structures and relationships. All participants stated that they were members of different WhatsApp groups that mainly centred around professional associations, community groups (every locality had their own group that was open to residents), educational groups for learning and groups that offered goods and services. For example, 'mata nagari' (good women) was a group dedicated to providing marital guidance/ counselling and offering child upbringing tips; 'smart cook' was a group where the admin would post recipes, which included pictures and videos, with instructions for improving cookery skills; and 'Ajin Malama' (teacher's class) was a virtual *Islamiyya* school – a semi-formal Islamic school – where participants were taught online.

Another key characteristic of many of the WhatsApp groups studied is that they are mostly female-only. The few exceptions were found among professional, alumni and religious groups as some of the members were male. From our interviews, a majority of women mentioned being more comfortable chatting and sharing information in female-only spaces. Cultural context is important here. The people of Kano are predominantly Hausa, the largest ethnic group in Nigeria. In Hausa culture women are expected to be shy, modest and gentle, especially when interacting with people.[5] In this sense there are certain topics and questions that would be judged as inappropriate for a woman to discuss in public or with people of the opposite sex even if they were in a family setting. This reiterates findings from existing studies that show women's use of ICT is not devoid of their cultural and historical backgrounds.[6]

Information is shared on the groups by different members and via personal chats. However, the reach of such information cannot easily be estimated even if it would be possible to measure this on the platform itself. This is because information is passed on by word of mouth to other women that do not have access to WhatsApp. Additionally, as most of information posted is forwarded either from other groups or from other social media platforms, it is very difficult to assess the validity or trace the original source of the information. Unlike Facebook and Twitter, WhatsApp is a closed network. Therefore, users are less likely to run into issues with government for posting or sharing messages that are considered to incite violence or chaos. From a political perspective we found that politics was a topic that was constantly discussed on the different WhatsApp groups. In fact, there were two groups being managed by women leaders from the two leading political parties.

These groups were not overseen by a central representative of the political parties but were personal groups that the women leaders used to engage members of their communities and to garner support for their respective parties. Nigerian politics is male-dominated. Although there has been improvement, especially with the introduction of gender equality policies at both state and federal levels, women still lag behind men in terms of holding political offices. Currently only seven out of 109 senators and twenty-two out of the 360 House of Representatives members are women.[7] As such there is general disinterest amongst women when it comes to political debate and discussion, resulting in low political participation of women across the country.[8] However, from our discussions with the women of study, it was quite clear that they were using WhatsApp in a variety of ways to improve their political understanding and engagement.

Keeping up-to-date

Many Nigerians receive information regarding government activities and updates on politicians through WhatsApp. Although the primary sources for information on government interventions are the websites and/or the social media handles of the agencies involved and media aides, women stated that they did not check these different platforms for such information. Rather, they relied on the updates that were forwarded to the WhatsApp groups they belonged to. For example, in one of the groups a member posted headlines from a major online news platform every evening. For many women it was not just about receiving the headlines but the convenience of having latest information at the fingertips, without the stress of searching for it. This meant they were better informed and could confidently engage in conservations about politics and the country at large. Even with colleagues and male members of the family as one of participants mentioned:

> Before when my colleagues were talking about things that were going on, I would keep quiet because I did not have much to say. After my friend started posting news headlines in our WhatsApp group, I could easily engage in such conservations. In fact, sometimes I would be the one to initiate and tell them something that they didn't even know.[9]

WhatsApp was the major source of information on politics and government for many women interviewed. The Buhari administration (2015 – present) has launched various interventions aimed at reducing the number of people living in poverty, tackling unemployment rates and boosting economic growth. Applications for such interventions are advertised using traditional and new media. Although women admitted to learning about the government interventions mostly from other people they would still make a post in their respective WhatsApp group asking for more information. This included clarifications about the application process, who had applied and whether anyone knew people that had benefited from the programmes before. Participants mentioned that this gave them a sense of security and increased their trust of the validity of the intervention. For many women this kind of post would spark their interest and seeing other women talk about applying motivated them to apply themselves. One of interviewees stated that the fact that other women had successfully applied motivated her to do so despite having prior knowledge about the intervention.

> I had learnt about the N-Power and TraderMoni programmes from my neighbours but I did not pay much attention to it till after I saw them discussing it in the group. I felt that if my friends are applying then I should too, it can't be bad.[10]

The statement above illustrates how online and offline interactions intersect and strengthen each other. Participants learned of these government interventions through traditional offline interaction. However, to verify and decide about how to act on this information, they relied more on WhatsApp interactions. The application facilitated fast and easy access to their trusted peers which in turn helped them to make a decision about whether to apply for the intervention or not.

Knowing who to vote for

In the last decade, Nigeria's political map has been dominated by the PDP and the APC. Although there are many other smaller parties, the presidential, gubernatorial and house of assembly seats are all split between these two parties. Both relied heavily on social media for voter mobilization and support during the 2015 and 2019 general elections. They maintained Facebook and Twitter accounts where they would post messages urging people to vote for their party and its candidates. In addition to these official accounts, individual aspirants maintained accounts of their own where they would regularly post their manifestos and comment on national, as well as local, issues. The goal was to attract as many voters as possible through participation and interaction.[11] While Facebook and Twitter were the most used platforms by the political parties and candidates for posting such messages. The pervasiveness of WhatsApp meant it was the most used channel for the distribution of the messages. Party members and supporters would forward the links or take screenshots of Twitter, Facebook and Instagram posts to share with individuals and groups on WhatsApp. This approach meant that in a short period of time the message could reach thousands more users.

From our data it was evident that these messages and videos that were being forwarded on WhatsApp gave women an opportunity to indirectly engage with the political parties and the candidates. In Nigeria, election campaigns predominantly involve large rallies with supporters coming from all parts of the country or state in which it is being conducted. A majority of women do not attend such events for cultural reasons, but with WhatsApp they were able to listen and see what was taking place from their own homes.

Another vital area where interaction via WhatsApp impacted women is voter's registration. Prior to every election year, voter registration opens – in fact it will be made continuous ahead of the next general election in 2023 – and civil society groups, religious bodies and political parties engage in powerful campaigns to encourage citizens to register. Messages, videos and voice notes are continuously sent to WhatsApp groups. Our respondents mentioned that constant reminders coupled with other members posting pictures of themselves registering encouraged them to get registered themselves:

> I didn't take the voter registration very serious but when my group members kept sending videos and voice clips of community and religious leaders stating the importance of registration and voting alongside their pictures showing their slip. I decided I didn't want to be left out.[12]

Beyond these general groups targeting citizens there are various WhatsApp forums that are formed by women leaders of political parties. These women leaders are female representatives of a political party in a specific electoral ward,[13] and they distribute messages aimed at mobilizing political support for their party. They deal directly with female voters and serve as an intermediary between the voters and the respective candidates or their party. WhatsApp forum provides an avenue for a woman leader to share updates about programmes and projects being executed by the politicians that are likely to benefit women specifically.

In our study we came across two WhatsApp groups that were being run by women leaders: one from APC and the other from PDP. The messages being posted in these types of groups were tailored towards women and focused on the parties or the particular candidate's intended programmes and policies for the socio-economic development of women. The groups consisted of an average of 160 participants and were very active both within and outside the election season. The dominant language of communication was Hausa with a few, mostly forwarded messages, in English. The members of the group were women from the same district as the women leaders. But these groups were not just used solely for political purposes; the women leaders stated that they used these WhatsApp groups to maintain a relationship with their supporters outside of an election campaign. They admitted to attending the weddings and naming ceremonies and paid condolence visits to some of prominent group members to reaffirm this connection. This was very important for the women leaders, as retaining their positions was dependent upon the number of female voters, they were able to mobilize for the party.

The second form of campaigning done via WhatsApp is by supporters of a particular party or candidate. Unlike the politically motivated groups described above, here supporters use pre-existing alumni networks, religious groups, community groups and so on to share political messaging. Our participants mentioned that politically inspired messages and videos were very common unless groups had enforced rules that clearly prohibited such. The majority of the posts could be categorized as being either pro- or anti-government. The women stated that it was easy to tell which category a person belonged to from the nature of messages. Political debate in these groups was more rampant during election season, when exchanges between opposing members would become very heated. But these debates helped other members decide on how to vote as one female lecturer explained:

> In the run up to the elections, I had not decided which candidate I was going to vote for, the debates between my classmates in our secondary

school alumni group drew my attention to a lot of things about the different candidates. This helped me to make my decision.[14]

Women participated more freely on these WhatsApp groups than other platforms such as Facebook or Instagram. In part this can be explained by the fact that WhatsApp requires just a phone number to sign up, meaning that an individual's identity and gender are more hidden. Also, the closed nature of WhatsApp groups ensured that women were often only in groups with people they already had a relationship with, and this enabled them to feel more comfortable about participating more actively. Despite this, the women still tended to be more active in female-only groups and more likely observe proceedings without saying much in the mixed groups:

> In our office WhatsApp group I rarely post or comment about anything. Unless it's a congratulations/condolence messages when they post something about a colleague getting married, having a baby or losing a dear one. The male members of staff are most active on the group.[15]

Increasingly heard?

Research conducted in other states of Nigeria has shown that certain cultural values have impeded women from participating in politics.[16] In Kano, especially among Hausas, continuous interaction with male non-family members is frowned upon and is often associated with immorality and bad family values. Interaction and communication via WhatsApp can therefore help women to negotiate such restrictions. Online, they can take part in discussions and even make valuable contributions from the comfort of their own homes, thereby avoiding such accusations that come with more public interactions.

Access to political representatives in Nigeria is very difficult. Many visit their constituencies only when elections are near. However, through different WhatsApp forums women are more able to directly and indirectly have access to their elected representatives. This is a potential seismic shift, as prior to the existence of such platforms, women would have to attend rallies or party meetings to meet candidates. One of participants stated that:

> Initially I always wondered on how to communicate with elected officers especially those of them located in Abuja. We only saw them during the election period but now this online group allows me to interact with them more frequently using the women leader as the intermediary.[17]

In previous elections in Nigeria, voting patterns show that voters were more interested in the party than the candidate. But in 2015, and especially 2019, voters showed signs of becoming more enlightened and unpredictable, particularly in the gubernatorial and federal/state house of assembly elections. Governors that were deemed unperforming and had failed to deliver on their mandate were voted out, despite the popularity of their party in that region. For example, in the northeast geopolitical zone, the APC lost the Bauchi state gubernatorial race to the PDP in 2019 despite its presidential candidate winning almost 78 per cent of the vote in the state. One partial explanation for this is that voters increasingly make their voting decisions based on personal experiences, online posts and debates, much of which they gather from their interactions on WhatsApp.

In Kofar Na Isa ward, Kano state women used the WhatsApp group to request that their state representative renovate the maternity ward of the local health facility. They felt that this project would have a higher impact than normal constituency projects that involved distributing motorcycles, sewing-machines and food items. In this case there was a general agreement on the importance of the project and after the message was conveyed to the representative by the woman leader, it was executed. However, this was not always the case. There were scenarios in which women felt that they were being ignored. They would make a demand through the woman leader and would not receive a response. They could even be removed from the group if they kept disturbing the woman leader about it.

Women use WhatsApp not only to interact with politicians and government officials but to also to come together and demand for progress. As members of the group, women are allowed to voice their opinion about issues in the ward that need to be addressed by the official concerned. Participants understood that coming together gave them a lot more power and meant that collectively they could achieve a lot. They noted that it was easier for a single woman to be stigmatized and labelled immoral than a group of women. The women mentioned that even their husbands were becoming more accepting of them taking part in political activities as long as it involved them acting as a group rather than individually. But even in such settings disparities remain. The influence of members with higher educational qualifications on group members with low education members of the group was noticeable.

The benefits of utilizing WhatsApp to engage with politicians and government officials are not experienced by citizens alone. For government officials WhatsApp has provided them with a platform to not only engage with citizens but to also monitor and evaluate interventions. Senior officers at the Kano State Ministry of Women Affairs and Social Development mentioned that they had previously relied on the use of traditional media, especially radio, to disseminate information about projects including the names of beneficiaries. With advent of mobile phones text messages and in some instances phone calls were used to contact successful applicants and to remain in contact with them through the course of the project. However, using WhatsApp, the officials were able to categorize women into different groups and create corresponding WhatsApp groups to manage them. Vital information about screening, meetings and distribution of resources was all posted on the groups, as well as through traditional means. The group admins would be the ministry officials in charge of that district and would comprise officials from different tiers of management. This approach has supported the timelier dissemination of important information. One official noted that:

> Before we had a WhatsApp group, a woman would show up at the ministry weeks after a programme had started or after we had distributed resources claiming she had not received any message or

not heard announcements on the radio. Resolving these issues were very hectic as some of them would start crying and there was nothing you could.[18]

For senior government officials the groups afforded them the opportunity to monitor their subordinates and to ensure that resources were distributed according to the stated criteria. Given that there are many cases of corrupt officers diverting resources intended for a certain project for their own personal gain in Nigeria this illustrates how WhatsApp can be a tool for accountability. One of the respondents stated she used the group to ask women about the packages they had received, their contents and the quantity. Some of them would respond by typing it down and others would take a picture and send it to the group. In a similar vein, another official noted that this was the easiest way to get feedback and to hear problems or difficulties that participants were facing in relation to a project, particularly in skills acquisition and learning projects. For these female officials WhatsApp provided them with an easy and cheap way of improving transparency of service delivery and fighting corruption within government.

Encountering falsehoods

Despite the many benefits of WhatsApp use and its positive effect on the lives of women, there are concerns regarding its use as a tool to spread fake news.[19] Users admitted to forwarding messages in many instances without knowing the source of the information or its authenticity. There are many cases where the repercussions of fake news have been severe. During the 2019 elections a multitude of unverified election results were shared and forwarded to individual and WhatsApp groups. In some places voting was still ongoing, whilst messages were circulating declaring a winner. In Kano state, PDP candidate Abba Kabir Yusuf was ahead of incumbent APC governor Abdullahi Umar Ganduje in results being circulated online, and this led to reports that he had won. But these results contained only the votes received by PDP and APC and were missing other vital information such as total number of valid votes and cancelled votes. After the final collation was complete the candidate of the PDP was in the lead with 26,000 votes; however, INEC declared the election inconclusive, following electoral law, because the number of cancelled votes was significantly higher, at a total of 141,169 votes, than the margin of victory. The state had to be placed under a curfew as reports of violence in some areas began to surface immediately after the official result of 'inconclusive' was announced. Many people felt that the governor had used government resources to steal the election and that the accurate results were the ones they had seen circulating hours before on WhatsApp.

Women interviewed for this chapter admitted that they were cautious when it came to forwarded messages and links being posted on the group. From our analysis, women with higher educational qualification were more familiar and concerned with the issue of fake news. Much of this has come through experience as there have been many instances where a member would post something and a while later another member would state that the story was fake. They stated that it was very embarrassing to be caught in such a situation. Other members would reprimand the member responsible and advise that next time she check the authenticity of a message before posting it on the group. One participant noted that:

> There was a time I forwarded a message and link about a Covid-19 relief programme from the government. It was forwarded to one of the groups I was in. I forwarded it to another different club. A member came out to say it was fake and even shared the link where officials of the concerned parastatal were warning people not to pay attention to it. I felt very embarrassed, especially when the admin asked that people verify information before they post it on the group.[20]

But for some women doubting a story meant not trusting the person posting the story which in most cases would be a friend, a family member or a colleague. There is a tendency to find it difficult to separate emotional connections from facts a finding also made by other studies on the spread of fake news through social media applications and WhatsApp.[21] WhatsApp as medium plays a lesser role in people's trust of the information being spread via it. Rather, women, tend to believe the information because it comes from a trusted friend, colleague or neighbour instead of a news outlet. This is another instance of offline structures and norms influencing users' online behaviour and practice.

The online–offline connection

In recent years, there have been many studies on the relationship between ICTs and the opportunities they afford women. This study investigates the link between WhatsApp use by Nigerian women living in Kano and its impact on their lives from a sociopolitical perspective. From our study, it is evident that WhatsApp helps women to access and distribute information relating to political issues and participate more freely. WhatsApp provides women with a space to share information on politics, interact with politicians, ensure transparency and engage more fully in electoral processes. The platform has supported significant changes in terms of women's access to political information but also their interest in the political dimension of society. This is reflected in how women convene for political discussion and collective action around government affairs. Additionally, the convenience of interacting with politicians online without having to attend physical rallies and meetings and risk being stigmatized was something they all welcomed.

However, their use of WhatsApp for such benefits cannot be understood in isolation of existing offline social structures. For example, segregation between male and female roles is a predominant part of the culture in Kano, and this transferred in to our participants belonging to, and being more comfortable with, female-only groups. The relationship between WhatsApp use by women and local social structures is influenced by prevailing context. Cultural norms influence how and why women use WhatsApp. But in turn WhatsApp is influencing and shaping a shifting of these cultural norms. Women are being listened to and are emboldened as group to take part in and demand for changes in issues surrounding their communities. Overall ICTs, specifically platforms like WhatsApp, are gradually transforming and shaping women's sociopolitical experiences in exceptional and potential transformative ways.

Notes

1   'The mobile economy West Africa in 2019'. *GSMA* (2020).

2   Savita Bailur, Silvia Masiero and Jo A. Tacchi. 'Gender, mobile and development: The theory and practice of empowerment'. *Information Technologies and International Development.* Special Section 14 (2018), pp. 96–104.

3   Varrella Simona. 2020. 'Most used social media platforms in Nigeria as of the 3rd quarter of 2020'. *Statista.* Available at https://www.statista.com/statistics/1176101/leading-social-media-platforms-nigeria/

4   Paul Adepoju. 2018. 'WhatsApp is finally catching up to African entrepreneurs with a standalone business app'. *Quartz Africa.* 31 January. Available at https://qz.com/africa/1194422/whatsapp-business-app-up-in-nigeria-kenya-south-africa-india/

5   Gbenga Emmanuel Afolayan. 'Hausa-Fulani women's movement and womanhood'. *Agenda* 33, 2 (2019), pp. 52–60.

6   Savita Bailur and Silvia Masiero. 'Women's income generation through mobile Internet: A study of focus group data from Kenya, Ghana and Uganda'. *Gender, Technology and Development* 21, 1–2 (2017), pp. 77–98.

7   Damilola Agbalajobi. 2021. 'Nigeria has few women in politics; here's why, and what to do about it'. *The Conversation.* 3 May. Available at https://theconversation.com/nigeria-has-few-women-in-politics-heres-why-and-what-to-do-about-it-159578

8   Emeka Eugene Dim and Joseph Yaw Asomah. 'Socio-demographic predictors of political participation among women in Nigeria: Insights from Afrobarometer 2015 data'. *Journal of International Women's Studies* 20, 2 (2019), pp. 91–105.

9   Author's interview. Kano. June 2018.

10 Author's interview. Kano. July 2018.

11 Oberiri Destiny Apuke and E. A. Tunca. 'Understanding the implications of social media usage in the electoral processes and campaigns in Nigeria'. *Global Media Journal* 16, 31 (2018), pp. 419–28.

12 Author's interview. Kano. April 2018.

13 A ward is a local authority area, typically used for electoral purposes. Nigeria has 774 local government areas (LGAs); each LGA is further subdivided into a minimum of 10 and a maximum of 20 wards.

14 Author's interview. Kano. July 2019.

15 Ibid.

16 Lere Amusan, Luqman Saka and Yusuf Babatunde Ahmed. 'Patriarchy, religion and women's political participation in Kwara State, Nigeria'. *Gender and Behaviour* 15, 1 (2017), pp. 8442–61.

17 Focus group discussion. Kano. August 2017.

18 Author's interview. Kano. April 2018.

19 Nic Cheeseman, Jonathan Fisher, Idayat Hassan and Jamie Hitchen. 'Social media disruption: Nigeria's WhatsApp politics'. *Journal of Democracy* 31, 3 (2020), pp. 145–59.

20 Author's interview. Kano. July 2019.

21 Esther Almenar, Sue Aran-Ramspott, Jaume Suau and Pere Masip. 'Gender differences in tackling fake news: Different degrees of concern, but same problems'. *Media and Communication* 9, 1 (2021), pp. 229–38.

10

Reinventing the newspaper for the WhatsApp age

Simon Allison

In February 2020, even before Covid-19 had been declared a pandemic, Tedros Adhanom Ghebreyesus – the Ethiopian doctor and former foreign minister who has led the World Health Organization (WHO) through its biggest ever public health crisis – issued an ominous warning: 'We're not just fighting an epidemic; we're fighting an infodemic'.[1] Sylvie Briand, director of Infectious Hazards Management at WHO's Health Emergencies Programme and architect of the WHO's strategy to counter the infodemic risk, explained further in comments she made to medical journal *The Lancet*:

> We know that every outbreak will be accompanied by a kind of tsunami of information, but also within this information you always have misinformation, rumours, etc. We know that even in the Middle Ages there was this phenomenon. But the difference now with social media is that this phenomenon is amplified, it goes faster and further, like the viruses that travel with people and go faster and further.[2]

Public health experts know that public health crises cannot be solved by drugs or doctors alone. Effective public health is about communication: getting the right advice to the right people at the right time, and convincing them to trust it. A vaccine is useless if no one believes that it works. Face masks are entirely ineffective if no one will wear them. That is where journalists like myself come in. They are experts when it comes to communicating information. This puts them on the frontlines

Simon Allison is Editor-in-Chief and co-founder of *The Continent*.

of the infodemic – and means, in these unprecedented times, they have a responsibility to find, package and deliver accurate information that is greater than ever before.

Journalism in crisis

Even before the pandemic, journalism was in crisis. All over the world, the industry's ability to act as a watchdog has been compromised by declining revenues, the juniorization of newsrooms and the intense demands of the 24-hour news cycle. The impact on printed newspapers has been particularly stark. In South Africa, according to the 2019–20 State of the Newsroom report, overall newspaper circulation has decreased by 20 per cent since 2018. 'Newspaper circulation is still on its downward spiral, with a few titles looking as if they might not make it,'[3] the report concluded.

Then the pandemic struck, and caused further havoc in newsrooms. It was no different at the *Mail & Guardian*, a fiercely independent weekly newspaper in South Africa where I previously worked as Africa editor. The *Mail & Guardian* was the first media house in South Africa to raise the alarm about Covid-19, repeatedly putting the pandemic on the front page well before its severity was generally accepted. During these uncertain times, more people were reading the *Mail & Guardian* – overwhelmingly online – than at any other point in the publication's storied history. In this new and dangerous world, readers were looking for information from places they knew they could trust.

Paradoxically, at the same time, the paper's revenues plummeted – live events, which made up 20 per cent of its income, stopped entirely, while few advertisers could still afford expensive print advertising – forcing the paper to issue an urgent appeal in March 2020 to readers to support the paper by taking out a paid online subscription. Lockdown restrictions made it difficult for distribution trucks to reach smaller towns and rural areas, meaning that fewer physical newspaper copies were sold. To survive, the newspaper's editorial and commercial staff all took a hefty pay cut.

As the scale of the pandemic grew, so too did the infodemic. Often misinformation came from supposedly credible sources: for example, some vets in South Africa peddled Ivermectin, used to treat worms in cattle, as a Covid-19 treatment; while Madagascar's president claimed that a herbal tonic invented on the island was an effective cure. It became more and more difficult to sort the important from the not, and the real from the fake. And if journalists were confused, when it is literally their job to parse, process and package enormous amounts of data, no wonder the rest of the world was struggling to understand what was going on. The sheer volume of information was overwhelming.

Imagine standing on the dance floor of a crowded nightclub. The music is blaring, the strobe lights are flashing, there are fire alarms going off in the background and everyone is shouting different things in your direction. And somehow, you have to make your own voice heard above the cacophony. That is what it feels like to be a journalist in the middle of an infodemic. It helps, of course, that the digital age – and social media in particular – has given journalists the power to shout louder than at any other point in human history. But many people now have access to the same tools, and many of them are shouting too. For journalism to have an impact, then, it needed to find a way of reaching readers in a quieter place; to somehow ensure that important stories would not be drowned out by the cacophony.

Harnessing the ultimate distribution network

'Can steam inhalation really cure Covid?' 'What about chlorine? Was the virus invented in a lab in China? Did Bill Gates release the virus into the world because he already owns the patent for the vaccine?' The sheer volume, reach and persistence of these fake news stories were troubling, even if they were often outlandish and easily debunked by journalists.

The stories had little to do with each other, and did not seem to indicate a cohesive disinformation agenda. But in the South African context specifically and the African context more generally, the prevalent fake news stories all shared one common thread: they were mostly spread via WhatsApp. According to a report by Media Monitoring Africa which tracked disinformation on social media platforms linked to Covid-19 across 2020:

> WhatsApp has the most complaints where the content reported was actually found to be disinformation (34%), followed by Twitter at 28% and Facebook at 24%. What the findings suggest is that the platform with the highest levels of mis- and disinformation is WhatsApp. This isn't surprising, especially when it is considered how easy it is to share unverified graphics and content – like audio clips of 'doctors' telling us alarming things.[4]

WhatsApp is the dominant online information sharing platform in Africa. As the Wilson Centre's *Wilson Quarterly* journal notes, WhatsApp is well suited to the continent because it uses minimal data (often WhatsApp use is zero-rated by service providers), works on inexpensive feature phones and lets people communicate across borders for free.[5] WhatsApp is subtly, but fundamentally, different to the likes of Facebook, Twitter, Instagram and YouTube in that it is far more private. Messages are sent from one individual to another, or from one individual to a group. These messages are, since 2014, end-to-end encrypted, which means that other people cannot see them. More private spaces are also more quiet spaces. If Facebook is the nightclub, then WhatsApp is the nightclub's private room – it's still noisy in there, but it is slightly less exposed to the entire world.

It helps too that, officially, the maximum number of people in a WhatsApp group is 256. This is in stark contrast to Twitter, Instagram and Facebook where people can communicate with millions of people at a time, and where every post is subject to being judged in terms of 'likes' or 'favourites'. Significantly, 256 is within the range of estimates for Dunbar's Number, which is the maximum number of people with whom one person can maintain meaningful social relationships.

In other words: people are more likely to know the people they communicate with on WhatsApp.

As a result of these two factors – its relative privacy and its more personal connections – people are more likely to engage with and subsequently trust information that comes to them via WhatsApp than they would if they accessed it online. That is what makes it such a good vector for falsehoods: rather than being broadcast to the world, it is spread quietly from colleague to friend to family member, each of whom is implicitly endorsing the contents of the fake news message and can even move offline, through the same networks, in this way. But if WhatsApp is so good at spreading fake news, why can't it spread real news too?

This is not an especially original insight. Media houses have been trying for years to figure out how to take advantage of WhatsApp's network, without success. Key constraints include the limits imposed on broadcast lists, which mean you can send messages to a maximum of 256 people per hour; and the inability to control who shares the content once it has been released, or monitor its exact reach. But there have been some successful examples of innovation in this space, with journalists in Zimbabwe leading the way.

Zimbabwean publisher Nigel Mugamu launched 263Chat in 2012, as an online discussion forum. He was fed up with the poor quality of public discourse in his country. At first, 263Chat concentrated on building a Twitter following, but soon Mugamu put more and more emphasis into creating conversations on WhatsApp. There were two reasons for this. First, Twitter was simply too public, meaning that state security agents could monitor the content of Twitter conversations and know exactly who was participating in them. Second, far more Zimbabweans had access to WhatsApp than they did to social media platforms, thanks to the special WhatsApp data bundles offered by telecommunications companies – these packages usually allow unlimited use of WhatsApp for a fixed price over a defined time frame. Among Zimbabwe's population of 16.7 million people, there is a mobile penetration rate of nearly 100 per cent and an internet penetration rate of 50 per cent. WhatsApp connections account for half of all internet connections in the country.[6]

Soon, Mugamu and his team were not just discussing content, but creating it too, and distributing via the networks they had created. By 2018, 263Chat was producing enough stories to create their own newspaper. But printing and distribution in Zimbabwe is expensive and politically sensitive. Mugamu had another idea, an 'electronic newspaper', with a masthead and page numbers and standard newspaper design, but with a key difference: It was published as a PDF in English and distributed via WhatsApp. Readers were invited to sign up to WhatsApp groups, and the newspaper would be sent into those groups every week. When a group reached the 256 limit, 263Chat would start an additional group. Three months in, 263Chat's electronic newspaper had more than 16,000 subscribers, and was on its way towards becoming a major player in Zimbabwe's media landscape – a position it has subsequently cemented.

Reinventing the newspaper

On 18 April 2020, myself and co-founder Sipho Kings launched *The Continent* as a stand-alone publication, linked to but independent from the *Mail & Guardian*. It is a pan-African weekly newspaper, presented as a PDF of thirty odd pages, specifically designed to be read on a mobile phone. The format posed considerable design and editing challenges. Page layouts had to be radically reimagined, with careful attention paid to font size and number of columns, with anything more than two columns becoming unreadable on a smartphone, for example.

Stories were also edited completely differently. Attention spans tend to be shorter on smartphones, where *The Continent* is often competing for people's time with Twitter, Instagram, Facebook and TikTok. An article that might run in the *Mail & Guardian* at a length of 1,200 words will be edited down to just 300 words without losing its essence. At the same time, it is important to keep the file size of the final PDF relatively low, because data is expensive in many African countries.[7] This limits the scope of what can be done with the PDF, making it impossible to embed audio or video which could further stretch the bounds of what is possible in this format. Despite the changes, it was important that it retained the design language and ethos of print publications – to make this look and feel like a newspaper, with all the gravitas that comes along with that.

The first edition – and every edition thereafter – combined first-hand reporting on politics, business and health from reporters all over Africa with high-end comment and analysis. The heavier stories are complemented by lighter pieces on culture, sport and travel, as well as plenty of photographs, illustrations and cartoons. Like a traditional newspaper, it is a carefully curated package of news that guides the reader. This is an important distinction from news websites, and the internet more generally, where readers have to constantly make a choice to read individual stories and inevitably gravitate towards stories they are already familiar with.

The first issue of *The Continent* was simply sent out on WhatsApp to the friends, family and colleagues of contributors and editors. They were asked, if they liked it, to share it to their networks, and to let us know if they would like to receive a copy every week. This low-key distribution strategy was a conscious choice. The aim was to target a small number of engaged subscribers rather than many casual subscribers. The intention is that these subscribers would themselves become a fundamental part of our distribution network, by sharing the newspaper with their friends and family.

The Continent communicates directly with each subscriber, via direct WhatsApp messages. It is also possible to subscribe on email or Signal, and a Telegram service is being introduced soon. Three days after launch, the publication had more than 1,000 subscribers from two dozen countries across Africa, as well as several subscribers from the United States and Europe. A year later, *The Continent* was the most widely distributed newspaper in Africa, read by an estimated 80,000 people every week in 102 different countries around the world. That circulation figure is a conservative number based on comprehensive reader surveys.

The publication has built a core subscriber base that is highly engaged and an active part of our distribution network: readers are encouraged to share the newspaper with their networks, not indiscriminately, but only with others who might value the publication, and survey data shows that 75 per cent of subscribers regularly share the publication with several individuals and WhatsApp groups. About 20 per cent of subscribers share the publication with more than six WhatsApp groups every week, greatly expanding its reach.

Initially, distribution was on an individual basis – *The Continent* would manually send a message to each subscriber with the new edition. This was time-consuming and laborious, but effective. Later, when numbers grew, the distribution team used broadcast lists, allowing mass broadcast to 256 numbers per hour, to send out the latest edition, although this is still a time- and labour-intensive process.

It is important to note that there is currently no bot or automated process that exists to make this distribution process easier. Attempts to engage directly with WhatsApp on this have met with resistance with the Facebook-owned company appearing to be reluctant to relax its restrictions on mass broadcasts, which are designed to prevent the spread of fake news, for legitimate media houses. This is a major barrier to entry for some media houses: both the BBC and Foreign Policy expressed interest in replicating *The Continent*'s distribution model, but were deterred when they discovered the limitations of the distribution process. These limitations are another reason why the publication has, counter-intuitively, worked hard to keep the subscriber base from growing too quickly.

Lessons learned so far

It is increasingly clear that news is most impactful when it comes from someone you trust. The nature of WhatsApp – which facilitates person-to-person communication rather than mass broadcast – encourages this. It means that every person who shares our newspaper effectively endorses it for us. These kinds of networks can also have an emotional impact: Anecdotally, we have heard repeatedly how families share *The Continent* with each other, and how it then becomes a point of communion between relatives who are not in the same physical space.

The second lesson is that the nature of *The Continent's* distribution makes it very hard to censor. Authoritarian governments can exert control over printing presses with relative ease; and have become increasingly adept and restricting access to websites. But thanks to WhatsApp's encryption, it is impossible for authorities to see who is reading *The Continent* or how it is being shared. In fact, the only way to censor *The Continent* would be for a country to shut down the internet entirely.[8]

This was especially important for our coverage of Tanzania, which had been a very repressive country when it comes to media freedom under former president John Magufuli. We were able to carry hard-hitting coverage of both the 2020 presidential election and the president's Covid-19 denialism that simply would have had significant repercussions for the writer and media house had it been published locally. We know from both our subscribers and from opposition leaders that our stories travelled far and wide on Tanzanian social media – shared in private WhatsApp groups and between individuals to evade government censorship. Zitto Kabwe, an opposition leader, said that the newspaper – both because of its content and because of its easily shareable format – made a material impact on the conversation around Covid-19 in the country; '*the Continent* is the most important instrument for democracy discovered in 2020. A balanced, objective and fearless weekly.'[9]

A third lesson is the power of WhatsApp to provide a direct conduit between the newspapers and its readers. Historically, reader engagement with newspapers has been in the form of letters to the editor. This is a very static form of communication. In the digital era, many newspapers have experimented with allowing readers to comment on their website. When this goes well, it can create an active and engaged community that vigorously debates the news; when it goes badly, however, it can provide an opportunity for offensive remarks and racist and sexist behaviour, requiring newspapers to invest in moderation capacity. *The Continent's* WhatsApp line has provided the newspaper with a different mechanism to communicate with readers. After the newspaper is delivered to WhatsApp subscribers on a Saturday morning, many readers will respond with their comments and feedback, and the distribution team can engage directly with them via WhatsApp. In some cases, a relationship is formed whereby readers use *The Continent's* WhatsApp line as a kind of informal fact-checking service, or to request further information on particular topics.

Ultimately, what began as an experiment to see how to distribute journalism on WhatsApp has turned into a full-fledged pan-African publication with a sizeable audience and unparalleled reach. In terms of producing the journalism, and distributing it, this model clearly works. The question that is yet to be answered is whether and how it can be monetized – and that, ultimately, will tell us whether the WhatsApp newspaper model can be more broadly applicable.

There are several revenue generation avenues that are already being explored. Advertising is the obvious one, and there has already been some interest from major companies with a continental footprint. *The Continent* has also attracted considerable attention from blue-chip donors, such as the National Endowment for Democracy and Open Society Foundation. It has raised nearly half a million dollars in funding over the past fourteen months, making it one of Africa's most successful media start-ups.

But *The Continent* has not waited around for funding. It has already published more than fifty editions and has featured stories by more than 200 journalists in a dozen different languages. In September 2020, at less than six months old, the publication won the prestigious African Digital Media Award for best news service. The judging panel concluded that:

> Placing *The Continent* on WhatsApp represents the bold thinking which these desperate media times call for – it not only exploits an existing digital advantage but also responds to a peculiarly African opportunity, i.e. the widespread use of WhatsApp among communities sharing information under severe government restriction. For a cross-border product, there couldn't have been a more suitable platform.[10]

Notes

1   World Health Organization. 2020. 'Twitter post'. 15 February. Available at https://twitter.com/WHO/status/1228683949796470784

2   Heidi Tworek. 2020. 'How a public health approach could help curb the infodemic'. *Centre for International Governance Innovation*. 15 October. Available at https://www.cigionline.org/articles/how-public-health-approach-could-help-curb-infodemic/

3   Alan Finlay (ed.). *State of the Newsroom 2018: Structured, Unstructured* (Johannesburg: University of Witwatersrand, 2018). Available at https://journalism.co.za/wp-content/uploads/2019/07/State-of-the-Newsroom-report-2018_updated-20190709.pdf

4   Thandi Smith and William Bird. 2020. 'Disinformation in a time of Covid-19: Weekly trends in South Africa'. *Daily Maverick*. 6 December. Available at https://www.dailymaverick.co.za/article/2020-12-06-disinformation-in-a-time-of-covid-19-weekly-trends-in-south-africa-19/

5   Heidi Vogt. 2020. 'Africa: What's up with WhatsApp?'. *The Wilson Quarterly*. Spring. Available at https://www.wilsonquarterly.com/quarterly/who-writes-the-rules/africa-whats-up-with-whatsapp/

6   Julias Thomas. 2019. 'WhatsApp has come in to fill the void: In Zimbabwe the future of news is messaging'. *Nieman Lab*. 13 March. Available at https://www.niemanlab.org/2019/03/whatsapp-has-come-in-to-fill-the-void-in-zimbabwe-the-future-of-news-is-messaging/

7   Yomi Kazeem. 2019. 'The cost of internet access is dropping globally but not fast enough in Africa'. *Quartz Africa*. 21 March. Available at https://qz.com/africa/1577429/how-much-is-1gb-of-mobile-data-in-africa/

8   Christopher Giles and Peter Mwai. 2021. 'Africa internet: Where and how are governments blocking it?'. *BBC News*. 14 January. Available at https://www.bbc.com/news/world-africa-47734843

9   Correspondence with the author February 2021.

10 Vincent Peyrègne. 2020. 'Winners announced for the African Digital Media Awards 2020'. *World Association of News Publishers*. 8 September. Available at https://wan-ifra.org/2020/09/winners-announced-for-the-african-digital-media-awards-2020/

Further reading

For those looking to learn more about some of the arguments made and issues raised in the chapters of this book, this brief further reading section provides a starting point. It covers research and media articles specifically focused on WhatsApp in West Africa but also highlights key texts that discuss digital and everyday interactions with, and between, society across the continent and beyond.

Ahmed Ali Akbar. 2021. 'Inside the secretive, semi-illicit, high stakes world of WhatsApp mango importing'. *The Eater.* 12 August.

Christine Mungai. 2021. 'We are just focused on being where readers are: Pan-African weekly The Continent publishes directly on WhatsApp and Signal'. *Nieman Lab.* 3 August.

Connie Moon Sehat and Aleksi Kaminski. 2020. 'Considerations for closed messaging research in democratic contexts'. *The Carter Centre.*

Duncan Omanga. 'WhatsApp as digital publics: The *Nakuru Analysts* and the evolution of participation in county governance in Kenya'. *Journal of Eastern African Studies*, 13:1, (2019) 175–91.

Ebeneezer Obadare. *Humor, Silence and Civil Society in Nigeria.* Boydell & Brewer, 2016.

Elena Gadjanova, Gabrielle Lynch, Jason Reifler and Ghadafi Saibu. 2019. 'Social media, cyber battalions and political mobilization in Ghana'. *University of Exeter.*

Elena Gadjanova, Gabrielle Lynch and Ghadafi Saibu. 'Pavement radio in the social media age: How misinformation crosses digital divides in northern Ghana'. Working paper.

Idayat Hassan and Jamie Hitchen. 2020. 'Forums of debate? WhatsApp and The Gambia's political transition'. *Centre for Democracy and Development.* April 2020.

Jamie Hitchen. 2018. 'The WhatsApp rumours that infused Sierra Leone's tight election'. *African Arguments*, 10 April.

James Yeku. *Cultural Netizenship: Social Media, Popular Culture and Performance in Nigeria.* University of Indiana Press, 2022.

Joseph Warungu 2018. 'Letter from Africa: Inside the gated communities of WhatsApp'. *BBC News.* 16 January.

Maggie Dwyer and Tom Molony (eds.). *Social Media and Politics in Africa: Democracy, Censorship and Security.* Zed Books Ltd, 2019.

Marina Lopes. 2018. 'WhatsApp is upending the role of unions in Brazil. Next, it may transform politics'. *The Washington Post.* 11 June.

Naima Hafiz Abubakar and Salihu Ibrahim Dasuki. 'Empowerment in their hands: use of WhatsApp by women in Nigeria'. *Gender, Technology and Development,* 22:2, (2018) 164–83.

Nanjala Nyabola. *Digital Democracy, Analogue Politics: How the Internet Era Is Transforming Politics in Kenya.* Zed Books Ltd, 2018.

Nic Cheeseman, Jonathan Fisher, Idayat Hassan and Jamie Hitchen. 'Social media disruption: Nigeria's WhatsApp politics'. *Journal of Democracy,* 31:3, (2020) 145–59.

Nwachukwu Egbunike. *Hashtags: Social Media, Politics and Ethnicity in Nigeria.* Prima Imprint, 2018.

Nyasha Bhobo and Kuakwashe Magezi 2021. 'This musician will sing about your enemies over WhatsApp'. *Rest of the World.* 10 August.

Rianna Walcott. 2020. 'WhatsApp aunties and the spread of fake news'. *Wellcome Trust.* 7 July.

Sharath Srinivasan, Stephanie Diepeveen and George Karekwaivanane. 'Rethinking publics in Africa in a digital age'. *Journal of Eastern African Studies,* 13:1, (2019) 2–17.

Sola Odunfa. 2009. 'Lies, politics and Nigeria's great rumour mill'. *BBC News.* 2 December.

Stephanie Diepeveen. *Searching for a New Kenya: Politics and Social Media on the Streets of Mombasa.* Cambridge University Press, 2021.

Stephen Ellis. 'Tuning in to pavement radio'. *African Affairs,* 88:352, (1989) 321–30.

Stephanie Newell and Onookome Okome. *Popular Culture in Africa: The Episteme of the Everyday.* Routledge, 2014.

Tactical Tech. 2018. 'The widespread use of WhatsApp in political campaigning in the Global South'.

Toussaint Nothias. 'Access granted: Facebook's free basics in Africa'. *Media Culture & Society,* 42:3, (2020) 329–48.

Wendy Willems and Winston Mano. *Everyday Media Culture in Africa: Audiences and Users.* Routledge, 2017.

Yomi Kazeem. 2019. 'Forwarded as received, WhatsApp is the medium of choice by older Nigerians for spreading fake news'. *Quartz Africa.* 23 October.

Index